Private Wings

... my life in logbooks

Dedication

To Joan, my high school sweetheart
and wife of 60 years.

Private Wings

... my life in logbooks

by

Paul Wallem

BANTRY
BAY
BOOKS
CHICAGO

Private Wings
... my life in logbooks
by
Paul Wallem
© 2016 Paul Wallem
All rights reserved.

The author welcomes your comments via email:
pwallem@aol.com.

Published by Bantry Bay Publishing, Chicago
www.bantrybaybooks.com
To purchase additional copies, or for large quantity
and retail discounts, please call
(312) 912-8639.

Printed in the United States of America
at Lake Book Manufacturing, Melrose Park, Illinois

ISBN 978-0-9850673-9-7

Contents

Private Wings

... my life in logbooks

> *I am alive. Up here with the song of the engine and the air whispering on my face as sunlight and shadows play upon the banking, wheeling wings, I am completely, vibrantly alive. With the stick in my right hand, the throttle in my left, and the rudder beneath my feet, I can savor that essence from which life is made.*
> — Stephen Coonts, *FLY! A Colorado Sunrise, a Stearman and a Vision*

Foreword

Ken and Lorraine Morris

We have known Paul both professionally and personally for over 20 years. We always look forward to seeing him as he invariably has a smile on his face, a positive attitude, and a kind word for all he meets. Therefore, we were honored to be asked to write this foreword.

Paul has been an ambassador for general aviation since he started flying. His many flights with non-pilots are a testament to his generosity and goodwill. Paul's stories reflect and echo what happens daily in general aviation around the country. They give you a taste of the many different ways aviation can affect both pilots and non-pilots alike.

Pilots always say that "aviation is a small world." (Actually, they say lots of things, and that is just one of them!) It is not uncommon to be flying across the country and meet up with someone you know in the most remote airfields, far from home. Paul mentions in his book that he got his first open-cockpit ride from Steve Thomas in a PT-19, the same airplane Paul later purchased. In one of those small world coincidences, Ken got his first open-cockpit airplane ride from Steve in the same PT-19 several years before Paul's ride.

A little story about Paul that he conveniently left out of his book: He can't sit still, and he doesn't really understand what retirement means. After his "retirement" from the financial planning business, Paul tossed around the idea of starting an airplane detailing business. In July. In an attempt to rid him of that crazy idea, we decided to get him started right. We gave him a big, greasy, dirty twin-engine radial airplane to "detail." Thus ended the detailing business before he even had business cards made.

Being professional pilots, able to fly all the time, it is easy to take it for granted. This book is a reminder of how fortunate we really are, and after reading about Paul's airplane adventures, other pilots will surely want to grab their own logbooks and take a flight down memory lane. For readers who are not pilots, it may prompt them to learn to fly and make their own memories.

Enjoy!

Ken and Lorraine Morris

Ken Morris
Captain, Delta Airlines (retired)
Aircraft Commander, EAA B-17 Aluminum Overcast

Lorraine Morris
Captain, United Airlines
Pilot, EAA B-17 Aluminum Overcast

*When once you have tasted flight, you will always walk
the earth with your eyes turned upward, for there you
have been and there you will always be.*
— Henry Van Dyke

My first plane ride was in this Globe Swift.

Introduction

Why do we fly? Is it curiosity? Is it the excitement? For business efficiency? Because defying gravity is different from any other experience? All of the above?

My first flight was at age 17 in a two-seater Globe Swift. It was exhilarating and unforgettable. I was hooked, but it wasn't until 20 years later that I began my flying career. After I bought a farm equipment dealership in Belvidere, Illinois, a farmer built an airfield nearby, which became the Belvidere Airport. I took lessons and flew for 40 years from that same airport. The name was changed to Poplar Grove Airport in the mid- '90s.

A few years ago, as my eighth airplane departed our airport with its new owner, I sat in

Each plane owns a piece of my heart ... I call them "my eight love affairs with wings."

my hangar and thought about what great enjoyment I had gotten from more than four decades of flying. I was 79 years old. Was it the right time to quit? My health was excellent, but I knew my reflexes weren't what they had been. It was time.

Thanks to the FAA Registry, I've been able to keep track of all the planes I've owned. I know where they are and who owns them. Why do I need to keep informed about them? I've wondered that, but I suppose it's because each plane owns a piece of my heart. Each played a part in my life. I call them "my eight love affairs with wings." Yes, I've kissed a few warm cowls through the years, as I hear other pilots do following safe and successful flights.

Recently, I asked two dozen pilot-friends what they first looked at upon receiving their monthly *Sport Aviation*. Nearly all of them said it was the first-person stories, describing events that every pilot can learn from.

So, in an attempt to pay it forward, this book is made up of adventures with each of my eight planes, along with a few mistakes on my part and some unusual situations. Three full logbooks, which include date of flight, destination, and duration, help make these stories possible. My hope is that other pilots will benefit from these experiences.

I've heard it said that airplanes are just machines. They are far more than that in my experience. Please join me as I look back without regrets, only with gratitude that I was blessed with possession of these eight wonderful flying machines. This is my opportunity to share special moments with you.

> → Rule of the Air ←

The propeller is just a big fan in front of the plane used to
keep the pilot cool. When it stops, you can actually
watch the pilot start to sweat.

The engine is the heart of the airplane, but the pilot is its soul. — Walter Raleigh

DATE 1977	AIRCRAFT MAKE AND MODEL	AIRCRAFT Identification MARK	POINTS OF DEPARTURE &	
			FROM	
8-6	C-172	1214U	RFO-SQI-	
8-15	C-172	9529H	RFO-JVL-	R
8-16	C-172	1214U	RFO-ARR-	R
8-17	C-172	9529H	RFO-DKB-	
8-18	C-182	52607	RFO-DKB-PLL-F	
8-22	C-182	52607	Bel - Stevens PT	Steven
8-23	"	"	Stevens PT	Be

I certify that the statements made by me on this form are true.

PILOT'S SIGNATURE_____

Part One

My eight love affairs with wings

The Logbooks

L ogbooks represent many things to pilots. They serve primarily as a record of time spent flying and training that can be used to attain and keep certificates and ratings. Pilots who do not keep a logbook may be fined or risk suspension of their certificates.

For me, as I look back over 40 years of entries, those books tell the story of my life in the air. Tiny details of various flights trigger floods of memories, taking me right back behind the yoke. And this book came about, in large part, because of these small books.

Logbook #1: The first entry on April 19, 1973 was by my instructor, Paul Cascio, as I started flight lessons. Seven years and 874 hours later, Logbook #1 was full. In it were milestone moments: my first solo, when I earned my pilot's license, when I attained my IFR Rating, and when I flew the first of my eight airplanes.

Logbook #2: April 14, 1980 was the first entry. Planes Number One (Cessna 172) and Number Two (Cessna 182) had been replaced with a high-performance Cessna T-210.

Although it took only seven years to fill my first logbook, it took 18 years to fill Logbook #2. The final entry was on February 9, 1998, with an additional 1,330 hurs, for a total of 2,204. Planes Number Four, Five and Six are in this log. They were a 1980 Cessna T-210, a 1941 Fairchild PT-19, and a 1953 Cessna 170-B.

Logbook #3: As I began this book on February 13, 1999,

there was a surprise in store for me. Plane Number Six, the afore-mentioned Cessna 170-B, would be my longest love affair: nine years. Fewer hours were being flown at this point because of less business flying. I decided to sell the 170-B and buy another PT-19, Plane Number Seven, and then back to another Cessna 182 for Plane Number Eight.

The final entry in Logbook #3 was about midway through the book. After accumulating over 3,000 hours in the air with these eight great airplanes, my final notation, shown below, was on July 20, 2012, the day I sold Plane Number Eight.

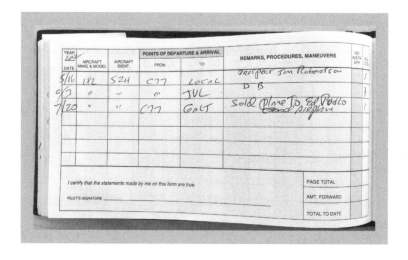

You haven't seen a tree until you've seen its shadow from the sky. — Amelia Earhart

The 1974 Cessna Skyhawk 172

Chapter One

March 31, 1974
I'M AN AIRPLANE OWNER!

What a gorgeous plane it was! A 1974 Cessna 172 Skyhawk with 200 hours. It was red, black and white, and I had just purchased it. My first passengers were my wife, Joan, our daughter, Linda, and youngest child, Stephen. I recall that I really wanted everything to go well and waited until there was a perfectly calm day without turbulence. I was very proud of my family that day. I'm sure they had some reservations about this flight, as it was their first time in a private plane. Yet, they were enthusiastic and seemed confident in me.

This was the first of my eight love affairs with wings, and while it was over 40 years ago, the memories of my first year as a pilot are just as vivid as if it were last week. I had soloed after 7.9 hours, took my flight test at 45.5 hours and logged 87 hours when I bought the 172. Today it takes more hours — and more money — due to added requirements. Back then, my check pilot, Connie Tomlinson, put me through the wringer with all kinds of unusual attitudes. After we landed, Connie said, "You now have your license. You can carry passengers." What a huge relief those words were.

However, deciding to buy my first plane was dramatic. It was a major investment, and I remember all of the rationale I used in convincing myself: "It's a business tool for our farm equipment dealership. Like our trucks and other vehicles, the plane will allow better use of my time — going after parts, going to meetings, showing farmers their crops from the air, etc." But in truth, the desire to own a plane started soon after I took my first lesson. I knew then that there would be an enormous amount of pride and satisfaction in ownership. The rental airplanes always looked tired and impersonal. I knew that cleaning, polishing and maintaining my own plane would be great fun. Being able to strap on wings that I now owned, to fly wherever I wanted, whenever I wanted, not just when a rental was available, would be true freedom.

But I knew I needed to justify the purchase based more on logic, so to my wife, employees and customers, I fell back on that first reason. "It was a business decision," I explained to them.

And, as it turned out, the plane actually was a great business asset. Quickly delivering spare parts to distant farm customers was a service that they really appreciated. Many of them back in the '70s still raised hay, and the hayfields made good landing sites. It also became apparent that the high wing of the Cessna, as opposed to low-wing planes, was an advantage on those hayfield airstrips, as there was no drag from high grass during takeoff. The slower stall speed of the Cessna also was a benefit on short landing sites.

That first summer of 1974, my 172 flew many farmers over their fields to see crop conditions. Those flights really helped to build customer relationships, and for quite a few individuals, it was their first flight in a small plane. *(Incidentally, I don't care for the term "small plane." They aren't small! The 172's wingspan is 36 feet. Most cars are less than 20 feet long and not as wide as the 172.)*

It didn't take me long to learn that I should avoid those field inspection flights on hot, turbulent summer days. Circling over cornfields created more than one airsick passenger. When they commented,

"It sure is hot in here!" they were really describing a sick feeling in their stomach. I knew it was time to land. Every pilot should avoid turbulent flights with passengers that are new to flying. It's a sure way to ruin any enthusiasm they may have for it.

Fast forward with me to 2016. I've been based on Poplar Grove Airport (C77) for 43 years, since my first lesson in 1973. Recently, Steve Thomas, our airport owner, called to say my old airplane was back! I'd sold the '74 Cessna in 1976 to a flying club, which was still the owner. It had been flown to our maintenance shop for some specialized service. I walked into the shop and there it sat: same color, great condition, with 5700 hours on it. What a thrill to see it again after 40 years!

> *When they commented, "It sure is hot in here!"... I knew it was time to land.*

July 10, 1974
BACK TO THE HOME FARM

I was raised on a farm near Ransom, Illinois, where I had some great times growing up. As a young boy, I rode draft horses bareback and set traps for muskrats in the creek. It was one big playground. But then I got old enough to help with milking at 5 a.m., and began spending countless hours under a hot sun in corn and bean fields on the tractor. Starting about then, my new goal was to get off the farm, which I did when I was 18.

Twenty-two years later, my brother, Truman, mowed a strip in a hayfield so I could land the 172 on the farm. It was 1300 feet long, and as I looked down on the fields I had cultivated as a teenager, it was hard for me to believe I was about to land there.

With full flaps and a slow approach, the strip was long enough. There can be only one first time for an experience like this, and it was a great feeling to come back home on my own wings!

July 11, 1974
"DON'T OVERLOAD IT!"

This was the advice from the old-timers on our airport. I never broke any of my eight planes during over 40 years of flying, but I sure did overload a few.

After having had the 172 for only three months, I flew to Chicagoland Airport, which today is covered with condos and is part of Vernon Hills, Illinois. The U.S. Navy built the airport to train pilots during World War II. An old farmhouse served as the airport office.

I was picking up three passengers, all good-sized men, one near 300 pounds. I forgot the 172 had a useful load of under 700 pounds with full fuel.

It was a hot, windless day. With full tanks and passengers on board, we headed down the runway for takeoff. As we passed the halfway point, I realized what was happening. We were too heavy, and there was no help from a headwind. To make matters worse, the runway was grass, which caused a lot more drag than if it had been a hard surface. With little runway remaining, I was barely above stall speed. I pulled the nose up, and as the 172 strained with every one of its 150 horsepower, cleared trees at the end of the runway with little to spare.

> *I was barely above stall speed. I pulled the nose up and ... cleared trees at the end of the runway with little to spare.*

If you feel that you are too close to gross, don't hesitate to ask passengers their actual weight. (Ask the men, at least!) Always put the heaviest passengers up front. That was a lesson early in my flying career that I will never forget. After that I was careful to calculate weight totals before each flight.

That experience also influenced my decision two years later to buy my second of eight planes, a Cessna 182 Skylane, which had a 230-horsepower engine and could carry more weight — big safety factors compared to the 172.

August 5, 1974
DESTINATION OSHKOSH

When we moved to Rockford, Illinois, in 1968, the Experimental Aircraft Association was still holding its annual fly-in convention there. I couldn't believe the countless airplanes in the air all day. In 1970, the week-long convention moved to Wittman Field, Oshkosh, Wisconsin, where it is still held. It continues to be the largest aircraft event in the world, with over 500,000 pilots and other spectators attending annually.

I decided to fly into the 1974 EAA Convention and, realizing I was still a novice, I read all the FAA notices I could find pertaining to the fly-in. That, however, did not prepare me for a sky full of airplanes, me being one of them! I was on adrenaline overload, but the event was incredibly well organized. I had listened to a tape of the prior year's controllers' conversations, and the discussion was one-way only, controller to pilots without response. Prior to Fisk approach, every plane is in line over the railroad tracks from Ripon. The controller at Fisk on the ground said, "Rock your wings, red and white high-wing." I did so, and he said, "Contact Wittman Tower." The controller at Wittman Field said, "Stay in line downwind for Runway 27. Plan to land on the green dot." On final, I could see that three large dots had been painted on the runway: red, green and yellow. They were each about 100 yards apart and planes were landing on each dot at the same time. Several planes were on final at all times. This was spot-landing in traffic, and while I did it again at other conventions, that first time is an experience I'll never forget!

To this day, the approaches and landing arrangements are similar to my 1974 trip. That has made it much easier to arrive and take off each year.

My advice to first-time convention flyers is to study the FAA notices and memorize them, because you will be very busy on arrival.

February 28, 1975
CROSSWINDS

An International Harvester dealer meeting was scheduled in Davenport, Iowa, an ideal mission for my business airplane. Instead of a two-and-a-half hour drive, the 172 would reduce the travel time to 40 minutes.

By that time, I had logged 190 hours. I was still an amateur, but confident I was able to handle most anything. The trip down that morning was uneventful and I landed at the nearby Bettendorf Airport and borrowed its courtesy car. The afternoon was a different story. I walked out of the dealer meeting in mid-afternoon to very windy and gusty conditions. This presented a problem, because although I had practiced a lot of crosswind landings, all were at or below 15 mph. I avoided flying in conditions with stronger crosswinds, feeling I was not yet ready for that.

At the airport, the wind was over 20-mph, gusting to 28, and was a direct crosswind to the runway. I settled down to wait for less wind. I waited. And waited. After two hours, the wind had only slightly diminished, and in late February, darkness was only an hour away. I decided to suck it up and take off. Takeoffs are not the challenge of landings in crosswinds, and I had called home base at Poplar Grove to find that winds there were right down the runway.

I got off the ground without incident, turned towards Poplar Grove and looked at the empty seat beside me. I had left my briefcase and coat in the flight office down below! I was furious with myself. I did not want to go back down and land in that crosswind. But after circling the Bettendorf field twice, I decided the time had come to land in a 20-plus mph crosswind. I was not going to leave those items at the airport and come back the next day to get them!

So, I set up a long final approach, with enough rudder and lowered wing so that I maintained heading. There was plenty of turbulence, and I bounced around a lot, but I landed. After my heart stopped hammering, I picked up the briefcase and coat, and took off again.

In a span of 15 minutes, I had accumulated two takeoffs and one landing in a crosswind that had kept me on the ground for two hours. That gave me a new level of confidence in my ability to handle a crosswind. As I later traded for bigger airplanes, a 20-mph crosswind became much less intimidating. But I will never forget the feeling of apprehension that day.

> Rule of the Air ←——

It's always a good idea to keep the pointy end going
forward as much as possible.

My second plane was a Cessna 182.

Chapter Two

CESSNA SKYLANE: THE WORD IS POWER!

I think back about why I wanted a Skylane. At the time, my Skyhawk 172 only had 400 hours and was in perfect condition. I had owned it for two years. However, a day in April 1976 changed everything. I rode in a Cessna 182, and it was off the ground in half the distance the 172 requires. The 230-horsepower six-cylinder Continental was smooth, fast and powerful. I knew I wanted one, so I started shopping.

For a month, I compared the larger useful load, the extra 80 horsepower, the 20-plus mph faster speed, and the larger interior, and knew it was time to move up. Steve Thomas, son of our airport owner, helped me search plane ads, and he found one in Ohio. The owner flew it over for pre-purchase inspection, and I bought it the same day. This became number two of the eight planes I've owned.

The next morning, the seller needed to get to O'Hare Airport in Chicago to return home. Steve suggested we fly him to O'Hare, with me in the left seat! The adrenaline really started flowing at this point. This became my first (and only) landing at O'Hare. On final, the controller kept urging me to keep my speed up. I was already at cruise speed and wanted to slow down for landing. When I wanted to slow down to 80, he asked me to keep it up at 110. When it was time to flare, the endless concrete made depth perception really difficult. It was like landing over water, and hard to judge altitude. We did get down OK, but now, many years later, I still remember the exhilaration of that experience as we landed at one of the world's busiest airports

During the three years I had this 182, I made 154 flights, about 80% for business purposes. Buying the 172 was a great thrill because it was my first plane, but the 182 was in many ways a better experience. It had a much larger useful load, it was roomier, and the extra power made short-field takeoffs safer. Airspeed was 145 mph, versus the 125 mph of the 172. Trip times were shorter. I really felt like the 182 was a more serious business aircraft.

Of all eight planes I've had, the 182 was my favorite.

July 5, 1976
BACK TO THE FARM AGAIN

Nearly two years to the day that I flew the 172 to our home farm, I landed there with my family in the larger 182. The 1300-foot strip my brother mowed in the hayfield was not at all intimidating. The extra horsepower made the 182 far superior on short grass strips.

August 1, 1976
BACK TO OSHKOSH AND THE EAA CONVENTION

I've attended about 30 of these EAA fly-ins through the years, and the earlier ones were much different. There was less corporate involvement, and I remember a larger percentage of home-builts and taildraggers. I undertook a side mission during this Oshkosh stay. With my oldest child Jeff (who had been a CAP member during high school) as a passenger, we flew to Mitchell Field and Timmerman Airport in Milwaukee so I could get more experience with large airports. The controllers were very gracious in granting touch-and-go practice at both fields. I used to be concerned about practicing at large airports, believing that the controllers did not want to be bothered with small planes. Later, I was told by a controller that they much preferred being busy and that the size of the plane did not matter. I'm sure that is different today at fields where heavy commercial traffic exists.

August 27, 1976

This flight to Indiana underlined the true business value of a private airplane. A mint farmer at North Judson, Indiana, called in response to our farm equipment ads. He was interested in two tractors and I needed to inspect his trade-ins. However, he was over five hours away from our dealership by car, and a round trip would have required a full day away. Instead, I flew the 182 to his farm in 1.2 hours, agreed on a trade price and was back at the dealership by lunch. Instead of passing up this transaction or spending all day in the car, I made a profitable trade and had a perfect excuse for a morning in the air!

November 6, 1976

November is pheasant season in the Midwest, and I invited two IH friends to join me on a hunting trip to Grinnell, Iowa. The only place to land near our host's farm was a grass strip at a neighboring farm. Grinnell is midway between Cedar Rapids and Des Moines, and wind advisories from both those airports indicated strong surface winds out of the west. We arrived at the Grinnell farm strip, hoping it would be an east-west runway. No such luck! It was north-south. I flew a low pass to better measure the crosswind. The windsock stood straight out of the west, and the low pass felt more like a 20 mph or greater crosswind. We landed to the north with the left wing low, as I have always felt more in control with the crosswind from the pilot's side of the plane. Remember my unsettling Bettendorf experience with the 172 in a strong crosswind? This landing was much easier due to the heavier weight of the Skylane and my increased confidence in crosswinds through the years.

The numerous mentions of crosswind landings is because of my frequent use of farm strips with only one runway direction. A large part of the time, these strips require crosswind landings. A pilot flying mostly from a large airport with several runways can avoid crosswind landings much of the time. However, it would be wise to seek out crosswind situations to build confidence for the times that you will face these conditions. You will then be ready when you do not have a choice of runway headings.

January 10, 1977
TIME FOR AN INSTRUMENT RATING

This was a flight to Minocqua, Wisconsin, to interview a prospective employee. As usual, the forecast received that morning for the return later that day was wrong. I flew up VFR in sunshine, but the forecasted VFR for the trip home had turned into low overcast. It appeared that no VFR conditions would be returning till morning, so I tied down the 182, rented a car and started the four-hour trip home. During that drive, I concluded that an IFR rating is a must if a plane is to be used for serious business use. If I'd had an IFR ticket this day, I would be flying home instead of driving and then having to drive back to get the plane. So, on April 1 of that year, I started studying and training for the instrument rating, which I write more about in Chapter Nineteen.

March 9, 1978
"SKYLANE 52607, MAINTAIN A PRECISION APPROACH"

Our irrigation manufacturer scheduled a national dealer meeting in Atlanta. With six months' IFR experience, it seemed logical to use the 182 for this trip. This time, the forecast for overcast weather was correct, and the entire flight was in the clouds with occasional rain. My logbook shows 5.8 hours going down, with one stop for fuel. The earlier training under the hood and my constant filing of IFR instead of VFR paid off on this trip. The arrival into Hartfield-Jackson Atlanta International Airport (ATL) in IFR conditions really ramped up the adrenaline. It spiked when the tower controller said to me, "Skylane 52607, pay particular attention to maintaining the ILS centerline, as you have a 727 off your right wing on a parallel runway." I still wonder if he knew just how few approaches I had made to minimums at a major airport. I never saw the 727, as he landed well ahead of me and was off the runways before I landed. I broke out at slightly above minimums. What an experience that was!

June 14, 1978
A GREAT DAY FOR SON STEVE

This was another meaningful event that happened because of plane ownership. Orion Samuelson, my oldest friend, has been the voice of agriculture on WGN since 1960. On this date, he asked if I would fly him to Urbana, Illinois. He was scheduled to speak to the FFA Convention in the University of Illinois Field House. It was my son Steve's 10th birthday and I brought him with us.

During Orion's speech to 11,000 members, he asked them all to sing "Happy Birthday" to Steve!

July 30, 1978
IT'S TIME FOR A TURBO-CHARGER

I was scheduled to speak at an irrigation convention in Denver. It was a 5.4 hour flight in the Skylane, and Joan and Steve went along. As with the above Urbana trip, use of a private plane often allowed us to travel as a family on these business occasions. We had a smooth flight out, but the following day was a different story. I hadn't yet learned to avoid midday flights during hot, turbulent days. From the moment we lifted off, it was obvious we were in for a rough ride, at least until we could gain some altitude. However, Denver is just over 5,000 feet in elevation and it was hot, so density altitude prevented a decent climb rate. At 300 feet per minute, we were not getting up there. It seemed to take forever to get above the turbulence. Joan and Steve were very quiet and slightly green.

Five months later, I replaced the 182 with a Cessna turbo 210 Centurion. That was the end of a slow climb rate, and thereafter we filed for higher altitudes and had better fuel efficiency.

> Rule of the Air ←

If you push the stick forward, the houses get bigger.
If you pull the stick back, they get smaller.
That is, unless you keep pulling the stick all the way back,
then they get bigger again.

Things I've Learned ...

Ask your passengers if they have been in a small plane before. If not, spend extra time explaining what will be happening. Assume they are apprehensive. I suggest the following:

- Explain that noise level will be high during takeoff and quieter when at cruise altitude. (Otherwise, they may think that the engine failed when you throttle back.)

- Describe the checklist you will use prior to takeoff to make sure everything is working OK. (It's even better if you show it to them.)

- Make it clear that you will not be able to talk to them between takeoff and cruise altitude, as you will be busy on the radio with tower, departure control or listening and watching for other traffic. As you approach your destination, explain this again. (Or use your "pilot isolate" switch on the intercom.)

- Spend some extra time talking to them about bumps in the air, particularly with first-time fliers. Just like rough spots on the highway, this disturbance in the air is not dangerous. They should be aware that, just like waves when in a boat, the air we fly in is not always calm.

- Before loading, I suggest a walk-around to talk about the function of the flaps, ailerons, rudder, etc. Many of my passengers wanted to do this.

- One last suggestion: Have airsick bags in all seat pockets so they are easily accessible. And keep a "Little John" pilot urinal or a "Travel John Pack" in your plane. Order them from Sporty's Pilot Shop or other websites. Believe me, this is good advice!

A typical courtesy car at a community airport.
(Just kidding, but only a slight exaggeration!)

Airport Courtesy Cars

C an you imagine walking into a business office in any town and asking for the use of a car, for free? And you want it for an unspecified time, maybe an hour, or four hours, or even more?

Small community airports do this all the time. During the past 40 years, I have often landed at those airports, asked for a courtesy car, and they hand over the keys. It's all free. Nothing but courtesy.

It seems to me that this, alone, typifies local community airports. I usually bought avgas from them, but occasionally, I had only burned off a little and didn't need to fill up. It made no difference. They still provided me the courtesy car.

Granted, these were not brand new luxury cars! It was always fun to walk out to see what I would be driving. Sometimes, it was a 20-year-old Buick with 250,000 miles, and sometimes it was something with more miles! Occasionally, it was as old as I was (or close). But it was always provided as a courtesy. I would always put some gas in it for the next pilot.

Small airports are wonderful!

My third plane was my first partnership.

Chapter Three

February 12, 1979
CESSNA T-210 N-732WX, A PARTNERSHIP

This 210 was hangared at our airport and owned by a friend who flew it less than 20 hours a year. I suggested that he sell me half of the appraised value, and we would form a partnership.

The arrangement worked out well. Our attorney prepared the partnership agreement, and his attorney approved it. I used it much more than he did, and we divided the expenses proportionally. Many pilots could benefit from a partnership if both parties are compatible and usage does not conflict. The fixed expenses of insurance, annual, and hangar are cut in half.

My first check ride in the 210 with one of our instructors was quite memorable. After leaving home base (C77), we flew a short distance to Lake Lawn Airport to practice landings. As I turned on final, I reached down to center the fuel switch. Both my 172 and 182 had left, right and "both" positions and the pre-landing checklist indicated that landings should be in the "both" position.

As I started to move the switch to "both," the instructor slapped my hand as hard as he could. I was stunned. He told me to look at the switch. Where the 172 and 182 had indicated a "both" position, the 210 showed "off" in that spot. I would have shut off the fuel, and because the air field was just off the lake, I might have ended up in the water! By shocking me with his actions, he did a great job of teaching me not to do that ever again!

May 22, 1979
TWO EXTRA SEATS ARE GREAT!

This family trip was only possible due to the six seats in the 210. Before, with the 172 and the 182, four seats meant somebody stayed home. Our daughter was considering attending the University of Minnesota at Minneapolis. We all wanted to tour the campus with her, and the extra two seats made that possible. It was a VFR day, and flying up the Mississippi River made this a great family outing.

June 30, 1979

One of our store managers was getting married 150 miles from our home in Rockford. Instead of driving seven hours round trip, Joan and I spent a total of two hours in the air. It was one more benefit of a business airplane.

September 14, 1979

This was the date for the grand opening of our new dealership in Plainfield, Wisconsin. Because the 210 had six seats and I had an IFR rating, I was able to fly to Palwaukee Airport in Wheeling, Illinois, pick up my close friend Orion Samuelson, and his cameramen and equipment. Without the IFR rating, this flight would not have been possible due to the overcast that day.

We flew to Plainfield and returned to Wheeling that evening. Orion's WGN Radio station reached out more than 500 miles in every direction, and his radio and TV coverage of our new store was invaluable. It was possible only because of the airplane. His schedule would not have allowed a five-hour drive each way.

November 20, 1979
THE 210 IS GROUNDED!

This wintry day had no overcast in the forecast, and the trip to Plainfield was VFR. By mid-afternoon, however, the forecast was entirely different. Not only was there low overcast for the trip home, but PIREPS (pilot reports) had reported icing in the clouds. I had to be back that evening, so there was only one choice: tie down the airplane and drive home. Icing has always been a major fear for me, and should be for any general aviation pilot. This was the only time I ever had to leave this airplane behind.

January 18, 1981
TROUBLE GOING BOTH DIRECTIONS —
AND A LESSON LEARNED

No need to look at the logbook to remember this flight! We needed to attend a tractor manufacturer meeting in Havre, Montana. The distance was over 1,100 miles, but was difficult to reach by commercial airline, so we elected to take the 210. Following a fuel stop, the gear refused to retract after getting back in the air, which really slowed us down. The FBO at Havre repaired the problem after we arrived, which turned out to be the first of two incidents on this trip.

Incidentally, while at Havre, the news centered around the release of our hostages in Iran, following Ronald Reagan's inauguration that day. Quite an event for the history books.

On January 20, we started home mid-afternoon, and our IFR flight plan called for a 10 p.m. touchdown at home. At about 8 p.m., the artificial horizon rolled over and died. Remembering the advice of Richard Collins of *Flying* magazine, I covered the instrument so it would not distract me and reported our problem to Minneapolis Center. This was mid-January, and it was dark, but VFR.

The controller directed me to Redwood Falls Municipal Airport (RWF), 12 miles off the right wing. Up to this time, I had engaged the autopilot during most flights. On this night, when the artificial horizon failed, the autopilot disconnected. As soon as I turned towards Redwood Falls, I realized how little I had used the liquid compass over the years! It is always slow in catching up with any change of direction, and I was zig-zagging as I tried to establish a steady heading. I suspect the Minneapolis controller was wondering what I was doing, but his vectors to Redwood Falls got us there. We tied down the plane and found a motel. The next morning, the FBO made the repairs and we proceeded home.

> *The lesson for me was clear: Do not fly every flight with the autopilot on 100% of the time.*

The lesson for me was clear: Do not fly every flight with the autopilot on 100% of the time. After that trip, I always flew part of every flight manually.

July 10, 1981
A MISSION FOR A FRIEND

Stan Lancaster was one of the best friends I ever had. When I returned to International Harvester Company after discharge from the army, he was my first boss. We worked together for many years before he retired to his dairy farm in Michigan.

On this date, I was at our Wisconsin store and received a call from Stan's wife. He had been injured in a farm accident, with serious damage to his eyes. No medical treatment was available near their farm, and she asked if I could fly him to Chicago for treatment.

I flew from Wisconsin to Escanaba, Michigan, to pick him up and as we flew home with his head completely bandaged, he never said a word. The pain really shut him down. Without a quick trip to a specialist, he may have suffered more damage. As it turned out, he did lose one eye. Once more, I was grateful for the airplane.

April 18, 1982
IS A BROKEN ALTERNATOR BELT AN EMERGENCY?

Joan and I flew four friends, Paul and Liz Hill, and Tom and Courtney Olson, to Dallas to visit friends. En route home, we were on an IFR flight plan, tuned to Kansas City Center. My instrument scan suddenly showed the batteries discharging, and I expected that meant a broken alternator belt. Center advised that we were just south of Osage Beach Airport, Missouri (K15). I requested permission to leave frequency, called Osage Beach Unicom to announce our pending arrival, and when I switched back to KC the discharge was too far along to talk to them. By now, all instruments were going dark.

The first concern was to get the gear down manually, and I showed Tom, my front seat passenger, how to pump the handle (about 50 strokes) to get the gear down and locked. Obviously, I wasn't going to get the green light indicating the gear cycle was completed. I just had faith that the gear was locked.

> I wasn't going to get the green light indicating the gear cycle was completed. I just had faith that the gear was locked.

As he was busy pumping, Liz, in the back seat, asked if we were going to crash! Joan was always good at reassuring our passengers.

We landed OK and I phoned the Flight Service Station to report we were safe and to cancel our IFR flight plan. We stayed overnight at Tan-Tar-A, a lovely resort on the Lake of the Ozarks.

Sure enough, the alternator belt had broken. The FBO had us repaired early the next morning, and we departed Osage Beach for home. As soon as we were airborne, I radioed Kansas City Center to re-open our IFR flight plan to Poplar Grove (C77). The controller asked if we had enjoyed our unplanned overnight stay. When I asked how he knew, it turned out he was working our flight the prior day when we had to land. What a small world it sometimes is!

At the time the problem appeared, I did not feel it was necessary to report an emergency. We were in VFR conditions, an airport was nearby and I knew we could lower the gear manually. I learned another lesson from this experience, however: I should have been scanning the instruments more often. If I had noted the discharge earlier, we would still have had power to communicate with Osage Beach traffic as we landed, and would have been able to lower the gear with power and get the green light assuring the gear was down and locked.

September 20, 1982
SOMETHING IS WRONG!

On this date, my son Jeff and I flew to Edgewood, Iowa. We had purchased a truck from the IH dealer there and Jeff was to drive it home. About 15 miles out, we started the descent, and picked up speed as a result. Suddenly, a terrific clatter erupted. Our first thought was engine failure, possibly a broken piston. Jeff is also a licensed pilot and he was watching all the engine gauges, which continued to read normal. Meanwhile, I was needing a lot of rudder to maintain our heading. Something on the plane's exterior was causing that.

I extended the gear, hoping to see the normal green light indicating down and locked. That turned out OK, and we landed normally, all the while with the banging noise continuing. With a great sense of relief, we taxied in and jumped out to see what was wrong.

Prior to 1980, all Cessna 210 Centurions had gear doors. Ours was a 1977 model. The right gear door had torn loose and was hanging by one hinge, banging against the fuselage right under our seats.

The lesson I learned from this flight is that every expensive sounding noise in an airplane is not necessarily engine-related.

One year later, I replaced 732WX with another Cessna 210, but it was 1980 production and had no gear doors. Incidentally, three months after I sold 732WX, the new owner landed wheels up, and damage was so extensive, it was totaled for parts. It is the only one of the eight airplanes I've owned that is not still flying. I still feel bad about that.

> Rule of the Air

The ONLY time you have too much fuel is
when you're on fire.

For my fourth plane, I went with a "motorcycle with wings," the open-cockpit PT-19. It was a great thrill to land on the home farm where my brother, Truman, had mowed an airstrip in a field.

Chapter Four

Back in the '80s, when our airport was still named Belvidere Airport, the fixed-base operator (FBO) was MST Aviation. Owner/manager Dick Thomas had restored a 1943 Fairchild PT-19 that had been in pieces at Machesney Airport. He painted it red, white and blue Thunderbird colors. It was a beautiful open-cockpit airplane.

One day, I made the mistake of riding in it with Dick's son, Steve. Before we landed, I knew I had to find a way to buy it. It was my first open-cockpit ride, and my love for motorcycles just got replaced with this incredible machine. It really did feel like a motorcycle with wings.

Dick needed a tractor for lawn maintenance, and I wanted his PT-19. I had a tractor that would work, so we traded. I still had the Cessna 210, and rented an adjoining hangar for the PT.

The history behind the PT-19 is quite a story. In 1938, industrialist Sherman Fairchild became aware that the U.S. military needed an American-built low-wing primary trainer. His company developed the F-22, which became the PT-19. He installed a revolutionary six-cylinder inverted engine known as the Ranger, producing 150 horsepower.

Fairchild built 3,955 PT-19s for the U.S. Army. Variations of the design, including radial engines and closed cockpits, brought the final production total up to 8,130 planes. Hundreds of WWII combat pilots learned how to fly in these Fairchilds. The planes ended up with the nickname "Cradle of Heroes."

During the six years I had this plane, I flew it to a lot of fly-in breakfasts around the Midwest, and to the EAA Oshkosh Convention each year. Many WWII veterans would stop by to tell me they had received basic training in a plane like mine. I loved hearing their stories about graduating from the Fairchild to a T-6, then on to a warbird, like the P-51. Some would ask to sit in the cockpit where they could think back about those early training flights. This turned out to be one of the bonuses of owning this airplane.

The PT was a joy to fly. Military aircraft use rods instead of cables to attach the controls, so a slight movement of the stick would provide the same amount of movement to ailerons or rudder. (Years later, when I flew a T-28, the controls had this same precise feel.) The PT was flown from the front cockpit, and the narrow Ranger engine allowed great forward visibility on the ground. The crank starter fascinated observers, as many had never seen this before.

May 2, 1982
MY FIRST SPIN ... WOW!

The day following my first spin in the PT-19, I described my feelings about the experience in a notebook, and saved it. Here's what I wrote:

There are few words in the English language to describe my emotions today as I rode through my first spin in any aircraft. Since my first plane ride in a Cub back in the '50s and after 1500 hours of personal flight time I have wondered and puzzled about the human sensations resulting from a spin. My private license training in the early '70s did not include spins in the instruction. Yet, the curiosity remained. The recent purchase of my PT-19 primary trainer caused a heightened curiosity about spins. I had discovered that spin recovery was part of military training during WWII. Yesterday, Steve Thomas offered to end my curiosity. We

One ride in the PT-19 and I was hooked. I had to own one.

took to the air and he initiated a spin.

Describing it is similar to explaining how to ride a horse. It can be put in words but it's tough to do. Here goes: Normally, you feel gravity in any standard aircraft turn. As a spin begins, however, the plane seems to stop and the earth starts a fast continuous turn. Airspeed is slow but constant, yet altitude is dropping. All the normal expected sensations of a turn have been altered.

As our spin to the left begins, I start counting turns. The horizon is in the wrong place. One full turn is quick, then another. It honestly looks like we are traveling straight down because the windshield is full of cornfield.

Time for recovery. The sensation creates a desire to pull the stick back, due to the close appearance of the ground straight ahead. However the plane is really in a 45-degree nose-down attitude, and back pressure on the stick would keep it in the spin. I am well aware that is not desirable. At this point, a wing has stalled.

Recovery requires forward stick and hard right rudder. The first increases air flow over the stalled wing, the second straightens out direction of flight. Suddenly, the spin is over. However, the severe nose-down attitude requires aggressive back stick to stop the dive.

My first thought? Why wait all these years to drain the fear out of this mystery of flight? The fear is replaced with confidence that an action in flight can be resolved with the proper reaction.

STALLS

Most new pilots hate stalls. I was no different. I overcame that by repeatedly initiating them. Similarly, the fear of spins vanished.

According to my logbooks, that first summer I owned the PT-19, I gave rides to virtually every family member, friend and customer that would say yes to a flight. Everyone loved the freedom and incredible visibility of the open cockpit.

August 22, 1982
A FLOUR BOMBING TROPHY

The third Sunday every August is the traditional breakfast fly-in at C77. Back in the '70s and early '80s, we had all kinds of contests. Spot landings and flour bombing were always favorites. I still have the flour bombing trophies that my daughter, Linda, and I won. The PT-19 open cockpit was ideal, and she would sit in the back cockpit and hit the bullseye every time. We would do a pass at 20 feet of altitude (rules called for 50 feet, but no one honored that) and she would drop the paper bag full of flour. Great fun!

September 5, 1982
OGLE COUNTY AIRPORT (C55), A GREAT PLACE ON THE FOURTH OF JULY

For decades, many of us from Poplar Grove Airport have been flying to the Ogle County Airport at Mount Morris on the Fourth of July. It's about 40 miles southwest of Poplar Grove, and the fly-in breakfast on that holiday is quite spectacular, with scrambled eggs, sausage, pancakes with all kinds of toppings, cantaloupe, coffee, milk and juice. What a spread it is!

Since I started flying in 1973, I have flown to this breakfast with every one of my eight airplanes. EAA Chapter 462 is based on this field. They usually have a fall breakfast, also. We taildraggers love their east-west grass runway.

The route between Poplar Grove Airport and Mount Morris passes just south of the Byron nuclear plant, and the open-cockpit PT-19 provided a great view of the cooling towers. I vividly remember flying to Mount Morris on July 4, 2002. The World Trade Center attack had occurred the previous September 11, and all kinds of security measures were in place, including restrictions around nuclear plants. We stayed miles away from the Byron nuclear towers that day, just to be safe. I didn't want any military jets joining us on that trip! If you are anywhere near Mount Morris on a Fourth of July, don't miss this breakfast.

July 30, 1984
AIR SHOW FORMATION FLIGHT AT OSHKOSH ... WHAT A BLAST!

During July 1984, we were invited to open the Oshkosh afternoon air show as part of a formation group of primary trainers, including PT-19s like mine. My good friend Dennis Blunt owned a PT-23 (same as mine but with radial engine) and we parked together each

year at the convention. The chance to fly together in a formation was really something to look forward to.

The day prior to our appearance at the convention, an Air Force Reserve pilot led us to the nearby Appleton Airport to practice formation flight. We flew low out of Oshkosh to avoid the incoming traffic. At Appleton Airport, we parked together on a taxi-way to receive ground instructions prior to our training in the air. The group consisted of Fairchild PTs, Stearman PT-13s, Bird Dogs and Grasshoppers, 12 in all.

Lieutenant Weinfurter (an unforgettable name!) called us together and picked section leaders. He instructed us on safety and to stay two plane widths apart to begin with. We taxied out for a practice pass, and what a thrill it was to be part of that lineup of old iron. My PT-19 was built in 1943, and every plane in the group was that old or older. The day was clear and cool. I looked at my son Jeff in the back cockpit with helmet and goggles, and it was easy to think back and imagine these same airplanes carrying student pilots preparing for WWII combat.

Our first pass was a pathetic disaster! The three sections were far apart, as were the planes in each section. We not only had obeyed the two-width instruction, we had doubled or tripled it. I wondered if a week of practice would make this work, let alone two days. On top of that, we had screwed up the traffic pattern at the airport so badly that the tower called our Lieutenant in for an explanation. After his half-hour session with the tower, Lieutenant Weinfurter strongly suggested we improve our performance or forget formation flying forever!

So, dauntless aviators that we were, these 12 strangers from all over the U.S. in our polished and restored old planes went back in the air to try harder. We did improve a lot in the following hours. The Lieutenant (who watched all of this from the ground) informed one of our group that he needed to close the distance because he was in Minnesota,

Getting formation instructions at the Appleton Airport

and the rest of us were in Wisconsin! If I recall correctly, that pilot felt very uncomfortable with this experience and dropped out.

A few hours later, in front of 100,000-plus spectators, the rest of us opened the afternoon Oshkosh Air Show. We weren't as fast as the Snowbirds, as close together as the T6 squadron, or as precise as Tom Poberezny's Eagles team. In fact, we actually looked sloppy when viewed from photos taken from the ground. But we enjoyed our airplanes, maybe more than anyone else in the sky that day. The freedom of flight was so real, and I hoped that if there was a next time for us, we would herd these old airplanes a little closer together.

Here's the final comment in my old journal about this event. The Lieutenant warned us not to be distracted by the huge crowd lining the runway. However, when we taxied into place in front of that crowd, it was hard to ignore them. I had never taken off or landed in sight of that many viewers, and really had to bring my attention back into our cockpit. That was even more difficult to do as we landed in front of that same crowd. All of you taildragger pilots know how easy

*Our formation flying practice didn't go well at first,
but we got the hang of it.*

it is to screw up a landing! Fortunately, we all got back on the ground
safely, in spite of the many eyes on us.

May 5, 1985
ROCKFORD AIR SHOW - AN EXPENSIVE DAY FOR ME

Three of us were invited to open the Rockford Air Show as
a formation. Ron Johnson (PT-22), Dennis Blunt (PT-23) and I (PT-
19) flew two passes over the runway, in that order. We didn't practice
ahead of time, and I took off slightly farther back from the other two,
which made a very sloppy-looking formation. In an attempt to close
the gap, I revved that great old Ranger engine well past its 2,450 rpm
max for that first pass. BIG MISTAKE! By the second pass, I was trailing black smoke, and by the time I got back to Poplar Grove Airport
later that afternoon, I was four quarts of oil short. A major overhaul
came after that, and I learned another costly lesson. Don't push an old
engine too hard!

March 20, 1987
AFTER 197 FLIGHTS, MY OLD FRIEND LEAVES

I was just starting a new business and could not justify the expense of the PT-19. I advertised it in *Trade-A-Plane*, and an Oregon pilot bought it sight unseen. He came to get it, and I watched him take off on a cold and blustery day. I'm sure he had an uncomfortable day in the cockpit, and I had a depressing day seeing my great old airplane disappear to the west.

This was the plane that made the centerfold in *Sport Aviation* magazine in February 1983. I never dreamed my love affair number four would reach that page! I had enjoyed six years with it, and didn't know at the time that there would be another PT-19 in my future.

> ⟶ Rule of the Air ⟵
>
> Stay out of clouds. The silver lining everyone keeps talking about might be another airplane coming from the opposite direction. Reliable sources also report that mountains have been known to hide in clouds.

*Looking out of the hangar past my PT-19 at my Plane Number
Five, co-owned with Orion Samuelson till 1986*

Chapter Five

September 12, 1983
DIFFERENT AIRPLANE ... DIFFERENT PARTNER

Plane Number Four, the 1977 T-210, had served me well over a period of four years and 190 flights. It was within a few hours of the recommended time between overhaul (TBO), and my partner was not using it much. It seemed a good time to sell it and provide him with his half of a realistic value, which is what comes from an actual sale. A pilot in Wichita bought it, giving me a few weeks to find another plane before I made the delivery to him. So I started shopping.

A 1980 Cessna T-210 with only 200 hours and located in Houston appeared in *Trade-A-Plane*. I mentioned in an earlier chapter that my longtime friend Orion Samuelson wanted to fly more often to his speaking engagements instead of driving. I called him, told him about this plane that was for sale, and he agreed to partner with me and buy half of it if I could locate a pilot for him when he needed to use it. I agreed to do that.

We ended up buying the Houston 210, and the owner agreed to meet at Addison Field in Dallas, which was about half the distance between Houston and Wichita, Kansas. The prior day, I had flown the old 210 to Wichita to the new owner, and my good friend Russ Anderson went along. We flew commercially to Dallas the following morning for a pre-buy. The plane was everything the owner had described, and we started home late in the afternoon.

The forecast was for VFR conditions all the way home. We filed IFR and were told of a cold front moving towards our route. We had sufficient fuel to go non-stop, which we did to stay ahead of the weather. This turned out to be the longest flight I ever took in 6184C, and after four and a half hours, we were home with almost an hour of fuel remaining.

Five days later, Orion saw our new plane for the first time. Orion used the plane a great deal, and in another chapter, you will read about "Air Orion" and how 84C is still in use 33 years after we bought it!

February 16, 1984
FAST PLANE ... BIG SALE

Steiger Tractor was one of the franchises at my farm equipment dealerships. The Steiger factory conducted great tours for prospective buyers of their large, four-wheel drive tractors. The plant was located in Fargo, North Dakota, 570 miles from us. The 10-hour drive (one way) was not appealing to our prospects.

Our Cessna T-210 solved the problem. At 200 mph, the non-stop trip to Fargo took only three hours. We regularly flew farmers to tour the plant in the afternoon, stay overnight at the Holiday Inn (with its blackjack tables), return to the plant for a morning session, and be back home that afternoon. On this particular trip, one of our prospects bought one of the largest tractors the day after we returned.

The six seats were a bonus, and the speed allowed the convenience of being non-stop. The 210 proved many times that it was a great airplane for business trips.

February 25, 1984
NO ICE IN THE FORECAST ... BUT IT'S THERE ANYWAY!

Throughout 40 years of flying, I encountered a lot of different kinds of risks in the sky. Thunderstorms get the most attention, and for good reason. They can be quick and deadly. My own limits were to stay at least 20 miles from them. The Stormscope in the 210 helped keep that distance.

My good friend Paul Hill joined me to fly to Kansas City Downtown Airport (KMKC) where I was to speak at a convention. The next morning, we arrived early at the airport to start home. The forecast for our route was overcast with no top reports. The only pilot report for the area was for turbulence, but it was 7 a.m., and not much air traffic was reporting. Conditions were 700 feet overcast, 38 degrees, dew point of 33, and light rain. An arriving twin reported a smooth ride from Texas.

We filed IFR and departed for home, and found a similarly smooth ride. Passing through 5,000 feet, we suddenly accumulated ice, and in a short time had a significant coating. Because we were light (only two aboard) and had a turbocharged engine, I chose to climb with the intent of climbing above the icing conditions. By the time we broke into clear skies at about 9,000 feet, we had a solid coating of ice but only a small loss of airspeed. I reported the ice to Flight Watch.

I would not have been able to maintain the same airspeed with less horsepower, and probably would not have chosen to climb if there had been no turbocharger. Once again, these advantages helped the situation. We were in sunshine the balance of the trip, but the temperature was too low to melt off any ice. When we touched down at Poplar Grove Airport, the ice fell off all at once. The runway looked like we had dropped broken glass.

We pilots do a poor job of advising Flight Watch of hazardous conditions. I have more fear of ice than any other hazard, because it is often unreported and not forecast. Thunderstorms are dangerous, but we have the option to fly away from them. Ice is more of an unknown, because often we aren't sure if we should try to escape it by descending or climbing.

Technology continually changes aviation, and in October 2015, the FAA discontinued the universal Flight Watch frequency 122.0 MHz for in-flight weather services. Weather services provided under the Flight Watch program En route Flight Advisory Service (EFAS) will continue to be provided via charted frequencies pilots use to obtain weather information, open and close flight plans, and for updates on NOTAMS and temporary flight restrictions (TFRs). However, pilots may continue to use the universal frequency 122.2 MHz.

October 3, 1986

This partnership lasted three years, and worked perfectly. Both of us used this plane a lot, and the partnership cut the fixed costs in half. However, I sold the dealership in the summer of 1986 and no longer needed a business airplane. Orion became sole owner, and we worked out an arrangement so I could use it on occasion and pay him an hourly fee. That also worked ideally for several years until I again became a plane owner, this time a taildragger. Partnering in ownership can be a great arrangement if usage does not conflict, and if partners are compatible. It is very important to have the proper legal arrangement in place.

July 4, 1988
FIREWORKS ... EVERYWHERE!

It was already dark when we departed Civic Memorial Airport at Alton, Illinois (now St. Louis Regional Airport). June and Wendy Godfrey, my sister-in-law and niece from Phoenix, had just visited family in Alton. Joan and I flew down to bring them to Rockford.

Plane Number One
1974 Cessna Skyhawk
Purchased: 3/12/74 with 200 hours
Sold: 1976 with 400 hours and 141 flights

In 2015, I got a call from the shop at Poplar Grove Airport telling me my first plane had just pulled in for repairs. It was such a treat to reunite with this wonderful old friend and see that it had been given excellent care. It was still owned by the flying club that bought it from me 39 years ago.

Plane Number Two
1973 Cessna 182
Purchased: 5/17/1976
Sold: 4/14/1979 after 154 flights

*Plane Number Three, a 1977 Cessna 210 was purchased 4/12/79.
I sold it 9/11/1983 after 190 flights.*

*Shown below is the cockpit of the Cessna 210. With turbocharger,
oxygen and retractable gear, it was a 200 mph business airplane.*

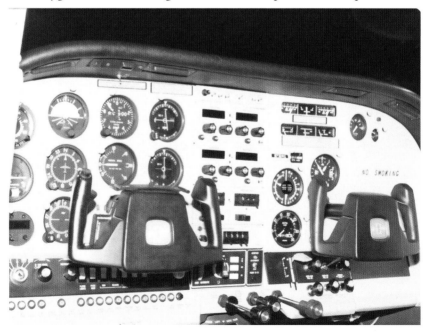

Plane Number Four, a 1943 Fairchild PT-19, was purchased in November 1982. Above, I'm flying with my son Jeff.

The red, white and blue Thunderbird paint job was rare on the PT. I sold it in March 1987 after 180 hours and 197 flights.

Between the time Plane Number Four went to an Oregon buyer and its current owners, Gary and Sarah Farley of Rice, Texas, it got a "new look." This paint scheme was the original one when the PT came out of the factory. The Farleys often display it at the Glenn Cumbie Museum of Aviation and Military History in Corsicana, Texas.

Plane Number Five — "Air Orion"
1980 Cessna T210N
Purchased: September 12, 1983
Sold to Orion: November 19, 1985 after 82 flights

Above, notice the black spot just below and to the right of the "C" on Air Orion? The gear doors were removed from the 1980 production model, which was a good decision. On my Plane Number Three, a 1977 210, a gear door came loose in mid-flight — with a terrific, alarming clatter. My first thought was engine trouble. It happened during a 1982 trip I wrote about on page 50.

Below, Orion Samuelson is flanked by his "Air Orion" pilots, Phill Wolfe (in blue) and Jerry Lagerloef. Orion relies on them to get him safely to and from Midwest speaking engagements and has said, "If my pilots don't want to fly in certain weather conditions, neither do I."

Plane Number Six
1953 Cessna 170
Purchased: 4/1994
Sold: 6/2003 after 357 flights

Plane Number Seven
1941 Fairchild PT-19-M-62A
Purchased: 4/16/2004
Sold: 5/6/2008 after 160 flights

A friend built a flying model of my PT-19.

My three convertibles: a 1941 PT-19,
a 1989 Harley Davidson motorcycle,
and a 1979 VW Beetle

The Cessna 182 was a great combination business and pleasure aircraft.

Plane Number Eight
1981 Cessna 182 Skylane
Purchased: 5/19/2008
Sold: 7/20/2012 after 296 flights

A statue of aviation pioneer Elrey Jeppesen, a gift from Jack and Peggy Wolf, provided the perfect finishing touch to our Vintage Wings and Wheels Museum at Poplar Grove Airport (C77).

The 2003 grand opening of the Vintage Wings and Wheels Museum, shown above, was the culmination of countless hours of work by dozens of volunteers. The 1938 Lannon Stone hangar in which the museum is located, center of photo below, was moved to Poplar Grove from the Waukesha, Wisconsin airport.

*Above, June 2003, Plane Number Six is
shown in front of our "new" 1938 hangar.*

*Below, the EAA AirVenture Museum in Oshkosh, Wisconsin, is a marvelous
facility started by Paul Poberezny, the founder of EAA (Experimental Aircraft
Association). His son, Tom, oversaw the building of the new museum in
1983. It features more than 200 aircraft and 20,000 artifacts, including
civilian and military aircraft of historic importance, and aircraft popular
with aviation hobbyists — vintage, homebuilt, racing and stunt aircraft. Jack
J. Pelton is now CEO (and vintage plane owner and pilot).*

Each one of my eight love affairs took me to the annual Oshkosh EAA Fly-In, now known as AirVenture. Many pilots pitch tents next to their planes, as shown above. Below, the large number of aircraft arrivals and departures during the fly-in week makes the Wittman Field FAA Control Tower the busiest in the world for that week.

H. Michael Miley

It was a clear night, and as soon as we began our climb, we started seeing fireworks. As we reached altitude, we could see fireworks in every direction, and as we continued toward Poplar Grove Airport, it seemed that every town in that part of Illinois was having its annual fireworks show, like they do every year.

The big difference was we were seeing dozens of them at the same time, and rather than looking up to see the beautiful colors exploding, we were looking down on them. It was an incredible perspective, an awesome sight!

Wendy had never been in a private plane, and the four of us had certainly never witnessed a Fourth of July in this manner, and we will never forget the wonder of it.

July 26, 1988
DON'T CROSS LAKE MICHIGAN ON ONE ENGINE!

When I first started flying, I heard that advice often at our airport. We are located on the west side of Lake Michigan, near Chicago. Benton Harbor, Michigan, for example, is straight across the lake from Chicago. The distance between the two is 125 miles by land, but only 60 by air. Pilots are often tempted to take the shorter route.

My concern has always been the poor survival rate in Lake Michigan's cold waters. The highest water temperature is in the low 60s, typically in July. The human body, without survival clothing, survives two to six hours in this water. The coldest water is typically in January at 37 degrees, and survival during the colder months is incredibly short.

I never wanted to trust my single-engine planes enough to cross the lake. It was much less stressful to fly around the bottom of the lake and be over land all the way. I always took that route when flying to eastern states — until July 26, 1988!

According to my logbook, I was to fly the 210 early that morning to take Dan Wilkinson, my good friend and business associate, to Detroit. As usual, we would take the route around the bottom of Lake Michigan, and return the same way, returning to Palwaukee Airport (KPWK). WGN Radio in Chicago had asked me to fly their sports reporters to Platteville, Wisconsin, where the Chicago Bears were holding summer camp. The reporters needed to interview the Bears at a fixed time, and I could see no problem picking them up on schedule.

I filed a return IFR request while on the ground at Detroit. As usual, I requested a route around the bottom of the lake, always over land. When I requested clearance, ATC advised that heavy traffic around Lansing, Illinois, at the south tip of Lake Michigan, would delay my clearance through that area for at least 30 minutes, maybe more. I knew the WGN folks had a tight schedule, and that much delay would probably make me late picking them up.

So I started rationalizing a flight over Lake Michigan, direct to Palwaukee Airport. I would be over water about 50 miles. I checked the glide rate of the 210, and decided that if I requested a high altitude, I could glide to land at each side of the lake for a big portion of the trip, and reduce some of the risk of a water landing.

How wrong I was! My plan was OK to begin with. I revised my IFR request to ask for a route that would take me from Detroit straight over Benton Harbor, Michigan, to Palwaukee Airport at Wheeling, Illinois. I requested 12,000 feet and was given a clearance for that.

By the time I reached Benton Harbor, right on the eastern shore of the lake, I had reached 12,000. Shortly after I had crossed the shoreline, Chicago Center directed me to descend to 4,000 feet! There went my "glide plan."

The adrenaline started flowing and I respectfully asked to stay at 12,000 feet. I was told to either descend as directed, or cancel IFR. I remember thinking hard about that. If I canceled IFR, I would lose ATC's instant reaction to an aircraft declaring emergency. That seemed like a security blanket I wanted to hold on to, so I swallowed hard, stayed with IFR and descended to 4,000 feet.

I estimate that my time over the water that day was about 15 to 18 minutes. It seemed like an hour! I don't think I took my eyes off the DME (distance measuring equipment) until I saw the Illinois shoreline. All the years before, I had set a personal goal to avoid this kind of risk. Somehow, I had talked myself into doing it anyway in the interest of time.

I never did it again.

August 18, 1988
THE WEATHER WINS

Orion's television show production crew, Bob Verecha and Phil Reid, needed to make a quick trip mid-day to Springfield, Illinois. I agreed to pick them up at Palwaukee, and take them down and back that afternoon.

As usual, forecasts were far from reality. By the time we started back from Springfield, a thunderstorm had developed very quickly west of Chicago, and when we were west of Champaign it had already arrived in the suburbs. We landed at Urbana to wait it out. Late summer storms are typically unpredictable, and this one was no different. The new forecast indicated it could stay in the Chicago area into the evening, so we stayed overnight in Urbana. An unplanned overnight stay could not have been with two nicer guys.

Endless stories abound regarding pilots who "HAD TO GET THERE" in spite of weather conditions, and died trying to continue to their destination. At times like this, I often remember these words: "I would rather be down here wishing I was up there — than to be up there wishing I was down here." The best advice for all pilots is to err on the safe side, and have great respect for the weather.

June 10, 1989
FIRST TIME IN THE COCKPIT FOR A WONDERFUL GUY

Harold Smith, my father-in-law, lived in Godfrey, Illinois. He had come up to our IH dealership to build cabinets, and I was flying him back home on this date. It was his first time in my airplane, and it was a solid IFR day. When we started our descent at Civic Memorial Airport in Alton, I asked him to watch for the runway and let me know when he could see it as we broke out of the clouds. I told him I would stay on the instruments until then. Suddenly, he said, perhaps with some relief, "You found the runway! It's ahead of us!"

Dad once talked of his earlier dreams. In the 1920s, small aircraft companies were popping up, started by whoever had a design they thought would sell. Dad was an inventor at heart (as his later career showed) and he and a friend had wanted to get into that business. But the Depression hit, and those dreams were replaced by the necessity of supporting his parents.

Dad's long career at Owens Illinois Glass involved numerous inventions on his part, including reconfiguring production line equipment. Because of that, the State of Illinois awarded him an honorary degree in mechanical engineering.

At a different time in history, I believe Dad would have been a manufacturer of airplanes!

1995 - 2014
THE AWESOME 4W RANCH *(and a broken wrist)*

Beginning in 1995, two close friends, Bob Kemp and Jerry Pitts, joined me on an annual mid-June trip to the 4W Ranch near Newcastle, Wyoming, where Bob and Jean Harshbarger raise cattle on 33,000 acres. For 17 years, we got on horses and helped move cattle. Jean's grandfather bought the ranch in 1924. It is the fourth-oldest Wyoming ranch, dating back to 1878. Bob Harshbarger was a Vietnam War pilot who had flown for Orion until he moved to Wyoming in 1987.

We flew 6184C to the ranch many times, landing on their airstrip adjacent to the house. The five-hour flight from Illinois would be 16 hours by car. We usually landed at Ainsworth, Nebraska, to refuel, and sometimes there would be no one at the airport. We would land, insert our credit card at the pump and fill up. I have always been impressed with the service and convenience provided by small, general aviation airports. Typically, we can land, use pop machines and restrooms, and even if we make no purchases we are always treated courteously and use their runways without charge.

During our 1999 trip with Orion, I broke my wrist at the ranch and Jerry, who had always flown co-pilot on these trips, flew us home. As a captain for United Airlines, his day job was flying 777s to South America, so flying the 210 was no problem for him!

A highlight of these trips was Jean's cooking. We ate really well!

Orion, Bob Harshbarger and Jerry Pitts with
84C at the 4W hangar

My two favorite aromas are from avgas and horse droppings. They remind me of airplanes and horses, and I love 'em both!

— PASSENGER COMMENTS —

I was a farmer when Paul was the local IH dealer and he would often invite me to go to fly-in breakfasts. We had a great time flying to Washington Island in Door County, Wisconsin, to the annual fish boil. We would fly along the Lake Michigan shoreline. I had great confidence in Paul's piloting.

We flew 17 trips together to the 4W Ranch in Newcastle, Wyoming. To watch the same landscape from a small plane is amazing. In those 17 years, you see many changes. What a thrill!

— *Bob Kemp*

After four years on the job as an agricultural advisor for the University of Illinois Extension Service, I went to work at Wallem

International in Belvidere. Paul was one of those people who could bring the best out in people and I was no exception.

Paul had given me the opportunity to learn the irrigation sales business and invited me to fly to Nebraska with him for informational meetings. I had never flown in a small aircraft and was a little nervous. I also experienced motion sickness easily. Paul reassured me that I would be fine.

The only other flight that was a little "thrilling" was when we attended a meeting in Iowa. The wind was howling and had I not had a lot of confidence in Paul's talents, this one would have scared me big time. To this day, I don't know how he got the plane on the ground. Even he expressed the difficulty with that one. I remember his popping the windows open after touching down to get a little fresh air in the cabin.

One of my most enjoyable flights with Paul was when he had an open-cockpit plane. I got such a sense of freedom flying in the open air.

— Phil Baylor

Tower: "Eastern 702, cleared for takeoff. Contact Departure on frequency 124.7."

Eastern 702: "Tower, Eastern 702 switching to Departure. By the way, after we lifted off we saw some kind of dead animal on the far end of the runway."

Tower: Continental 635, cleared for takeoff behind Eastern 702. Contact Departure on frequency 124.7. Did you copy that report from Eastern 702?"

Continental 635: "Continental 635, cleared for takeoff, roger. And yes, we copied Eastern. We've already notified our caterers."

I kept this 170 the longest of all my planes: nine years and 357 flights. It was beautiful, fun to fly, and easy on fuel.

Chapter Six

THERE ARE TIMES WHEN YOU JUST CAN'T SAY NO

After Orion Samuelson bought out my interest in the Cessna 210 partnership, I continued to rent it from him for occasional flights, and also got hooked on a rental J-3 Cub. Flying with the windows down is a great way to spend a summer evening, and my logbook says I flew it 17 times. Our airport has rented this same Cub (6673H) for almost 25 years, and it is a legend around Poplar Grove Airport, still flying whenever the weather is decent.

On this day in April, however, Scott Hartwig told me a pristine Cessna 170 was for sale. He thought I should look at it because it was the same color as my hair — gray! I drove to the Janesville Airport, opened the hangar door, and knew instantly that this was going to be love affair with Plane Number Six. Owner Larry Wixom flew it to Poplar Grove the next day for the pre-buy and then it was mine.

Back in the late '40s and early '50s, the Cessna 170 was sold in large numbers as a business and personal aircraft. In 1956, Cessna added a nose wheel to make it a tricycle gear, and that became the 172 Skyhawk. Over 43,000 have been sold, making it the most-manufactured general aviation aircraft of all time.

But I digress! Let's talk more about the 170 I had just purchased.

At this point, I had logged several hundred hours of taildragger time in my previous Fairchild PT-19 (love affair number four). But from the first day, my new taildragger was a challenge for me to land. The PT-19 would settle easily to the runway in a three-point landing. The 170 would touch down and then bounce right back in the air! Sometimes, I landed two or three times in a few seconds!

I finally got it figured out. The 170 has a stall speed of 54 mph. My newest acquisition, however, had a stall kit, lowering the stall well down into the 40s. Unless I slowed it down much more than I was accustomed to in the Fairchild, the spring gear on the 170 would put me right back in the air. I finally learned to slow it down.

According to my logbook, I started grading my landings at this point. I'm sitting here now looking at a lot of grades of "C," a few were "D"s and very few "A"s. Finally, the grades improved. Then I had breakfast with a Delta captain who also had a 170. He had the same trouble when he first got his, and I immediately felt better.

July 22, 1995
A BIG DAY! MY GRANDDAUGHTERS BECOME YOUNG EAGLES

The EAA Young Eagles Program was well underway by 1995. Their goal was to give one million youngsters a chance to experience a flight. My granddaughters Lindsey and Lauren flew with me in the 170 on this date, and became Young Eagles.

As I write this many years later, the hugely successful Young Eagles Program has surpassed 1.9 million young pilots. I have greatly enjoyed flying some of these kids, a little over 50 total. Nothing can be better than giving kids their first airplane ride. Jumping ahead in my logbook, an entry on August 17, 1996, shows eight participants flew with me on their first flight in a private aircraft. They tried to act cool,

*The EAA Young Eagles program has been a
wonderful way to introduce young
people to the joy of flying.*

but at the same time, they were so excited. I would have the front seat passenger take the controls, suggest that they keep their eye on the horizon and fly straight and level. Often they did a good job at that. After we land, they get their EAA Young Eagles certificate. I guess I've been around a long time, because some of my first Young Eagles are now with the airlines!

December 17, 1995
THIS GADGET IS MADDENING!

Many pilots love gadgets. I don't. The Loran in the 170 was said to be simple to use, but not for me. Then in 1995 Garmin introduced their new GPS (global positioning satellite) and their ad said it would keep me from getting lost. Sounded like good insurance, so I bought one. My logbook says I used it for the first time on this date.

I still remember that it nearly drove me nuts for awhile. I kept pushing the wrong buttons, scared that I was going to break it. Finally I mastered it, and headings, arrival time, alternate airports, etc., were all right there on the yoke. Most pilots today consider a GPS a necessity. Back in 1995, it was a luxury. I'm still all thumbs when it comes to new gadgets, however. I just replaced my smart phone, and after a week this one is still driving me nuts.

February 10, 1996
WATCHING FOR A LANDING SITE

The 170 engine was reaching high hours, and I was conscious of that. I found myself looking for a landing site when over a populated area.

So it was time to spend some serious money. The $12,000 overhaul was perfectly done. Our engine shop at Poplar Grove Airport is second to none, and even engines from as far away as Alaska are shipped here to be rebuilt. After mine was done, I felt a lot safer in the air.

June 15, 1996
AN UNEXPECTED LOOP

A loop in the air is planned, then executed. A ground loop is a different event entirely, and certainly not planned. En route home from the southeast, the dark clouds north of the airport were still a few miles out, but the wind was picking up. Remember what I said earlier about crosswind landings? I much prefer the wind be from the pilot's side. On this day, I broke that rule, because I wanted to get on the ground quickly, ahead of the rain. I landed on 27, which is grass, with the crosswind from my right. I didn't have the right wing low enough, didn't have enough rudder in, and suddenly the 170 was heading in a different direction. I wasn't sure what had happened until I thought about it for a moment. I had just experienced a ground loop!

Fortunately, no damage occurred, and I was lucky to be on a

grass runway. No one saw the event, so now I'll tell about it, and you are the first to know!

July 13, 1996
YOU MEAN NOW WE CAN TALK TO EACH OTHER?

During this flight, my good friend Dick Grassfield was in the right seat of the 170 and we talked with normal tone of voice, without removing our headsets. If you had not flown before 1996 you would say, "So what?" This was my first flight using the newly available voice-activated aircraft intercom. It was liberation day!

In the past, we would always remove our headsets to talk to passengers. Now we could keep the headsets on and still talk to each other, all the while monitoring traffic or controller calls. This was a milestone. It sort of reminded me of when I was seven years old and we first got electricity on our farm. What an exciting day that was! So was this one!

September 11, 1996
ROUTINE — BUT ALWAYS A THRILL

Night flying has always given me a special thrill. Night landing practice is required to stay current. On this particular autumn night, I booked three landings. It was a clear and cool night, and the ground lights sparkled like they do on a cold winter night. My logbook grades for this practice session were "B," "C" and "A." At least I got one "A" out of the group. I looked forward in the logbook and found that it was February 2, 1997, before I next had an "A" grade on night landings. The 170's spring landing gear sure kept me humble!

September 11, 1997
CESSNA 170B WINS AN AWARD

EAA Chapter 410 has hosted some great fly-ins at Whiteside

County Airport (SQI). On this day, my Cessna 170 was awarded a beautiful plaque.

It's an honor when others think highly of your plane. Maybe after looking at the color photos of 1932 Charley in this book, you will agree it was (and still is) a gorgeous airplane.

November 18, 1998
SPEAKING OF SLOW FLIGHT—-THIS WAS REALLY SLOW FLIGHT!

Poplar Grove Airport adjoins Route 76, which is north-south along the western border of the airport. Imagine if you were driving on the highway, and saw a plane above you going much slower than your car.

This was great fun with the 170, on the occasion when a really strong wind was coming out of the north. I could slow the plane down to 40 with flaps out, and a 20 or 25 mph headwind would slow me down to a ground speed below 20. I recall a day when the GPS showed ground speed under 10! Often a few Cubs would be doing the same thing, and they were slower yet. Once in a while, we would see a car pull off to the side of the road so they could get out and watch.

We were younger then. Some Sunday afternoons were a lot of fun at our airport. We didn't have as busy a traffic pattern in those days. Now over 400 planes call our airport home.

February 9, 1999
BOB COLLINS

Thanks to my close friend Orion Samuelson, I made a new friend in the early '80s. Bob Collins had become a favorite on Chicago's WGN Radio, and he liked to come to our IH dealership with Orion and drive farm equipment. He was not yet a pilot, but enjoyed flying with Orion and me in the Cessna 210 we owned together.

A few years later, he learned to fly at Waukegan (UGN), purchased a Bonanza, and then replaced it with an aerobatic Zlin. I recall the first time I flew with him in the Zlin and commented that the visibility was spectacular, due to the bubble canopy.

On this date, February 9, 1999, I flew to Waukegan. Bob had asked to fly my 170 to try and improve his tailwheel landings. He knew I had struggled with them when I got the 170, and he was having the same problem with the Zlin. According to my logbook, he did three landings in the right seat and they were OK. Later that year, he also purchased a new Cessna Skylane with a state-of-the-art collision avoidance system (CAS).

February 8, 2000
A YEAR AND A DAY LATER - A LOST FRIEND

On this February day, Bob was returning to Waukegan Airport in his Zlin. On final, a student in a Cessna 172 (high-wing) collided with the low-wing Zlin. Neither pilot saw the other. Bob, his passenger,

Bob Collins, shown with me in 1999, was a generous donor to, and enthusiastic supporter of, the Wings and Wheels Museum at Poplar Grove Airport.

and the student pilot in the Cessna all died. The irony of this event will stay with me forever. Down below in Bob's hangar sat the Skylane with collision avoidance. Very likely, he would still be here today if he had been flying the 182 instead of the Zlin. After Bob's death, I purchased a CAS and believe it is the best life insurance a pilot can have.

There is a lesson for all of us pilots to learn from Bob's incident: A low-wing plane descending near a high-wing aircraft means that neither pilot may see each other. Eyes outside the cockpit are so very important. Through the years, whenever we approached the airport to land, I've asked passengers to help watch for other planes.

One final memory concludes this story of a lost friend. Several years after Bob's death, my next door hangar neighbor Chad Dubbs bought a 1999 Cessna Skylane, complete with CAS.

It was Bob's old airplane.

September 4, 1999
ONE OF THOSE SPECIAL MOMENTS

I planned to meet another pilot for breakfast at the CAVU Cafe on Janesville Airport (JVL). The cafe had been a great spot, where all the breakfasters can admire planes taxiing in near the front door.

When I was flying the red, white and blue PT-19 open cockpit, I tried not to look too cool as I parked it and walked into the cafe, but every time, someone asked what kind of plane it was. With that paint job, it just couldn't be ignored. The restaurant is closed now. Too bad.

Anyway, on this day in 1999 when I arrived at my hangar to fly the 170, the visibility was at most a half mile in fog. Weather at Rockford Airport indicated clear above the fog. I filed IFR and departed. At about 300 feet AGL, I broke out and it was a beautiful, clear and sunny day. Penetrating through the fog was the top of a grain elevator, and near Janesville a factory smokestack stood all by itself above the fog layer. It was one of those special moments and I wished others were with me to share it.

This was one of those times when I was grateful to have the instrument rating. Otherwise, I would have stayed on the ground till the fog cleared, and I would have missed an awesome sight. Taking off in murky conditions to then break into the clear is just a great experience.

November 9, 1999
I WAS FINE. HOME BASE DIDN'T THINK SO.

En route home from Kansas City on a VFR flight plan, a SIG-MET was broadcast indicating a fast-moving front would be crossing my path 20 miles ahead. I canceled my VFR flight plan and landed at Mount Pleasant, Iowa (MPZ) to wait until the coast was clear. After about 90 minutes, the route was clear, but several pilots were waiting to file a flight plan so I departed for home without filing.

When I landed at Poplar Grove, one of my favorite people in all of aviation, airport co-owner Tina Thomas, ran out and gave me a hug. Seems like Flight Service had not canceled my earlier flight plan and had called home base to see if I had showed up. Tina thought I had gone down. It was the only time in my years of flying that Flight Service did not cancel as requested.

You may correctly say that I should have waited my turn and filed a new flight plan out of Mt. Pleasant. Remember, I said earlier that I would write about my mistakes in this book right along with the other stories!

April 27, 2000
WATCH OUT FOR GOOD DEEDS

I learned long ago that boats and airplanes need to be parked by their owners, or by trained line boys. This time I let my guard down and paid dearly.

Two good friends took a ride with me in the 170. After we landed, I was about to push the plane into the T-hangar when they decided to help, so one got on each wing and started pushing. Remember, the 170 was a taildragger. The person on the left wing stopped for some reason, and the other one kept pushing. I was at the tail, guiding from there, and suddenly the tail crunched against the hangar wall.

The result was an $800 repair bill. And you can't get angry with friends who thought they were helping! After that, I was more careful about accepting help.

June 27, 2003
IS IT TIME TO MOVE ON TO PLANE NUMBER SEVEN?

By this date, I had flown the 170 for nine years, longer than any of my other wings. There are 357 flights recorded in my logbooks, and it was still great fun to fly the plane. Our financial planning practice required very little business travel, so most of the 170 flying was for personal reasons.

I couldn't get the thought of another open-cockpit plane out of my mind. I had such good memories of the PT-19 that I started looking in *Trade-A-Plane* to see if any were listed. (WARNING: It's always dangerous to start looking in this magazine. It's like walking through a candy store.)

It seemed like a good idea to try selling the 170 first. Shortly after I advertised it, a couple from Owatonna, Minnesota, flew down, liked it, and took it home. I watched it take off on 30, and said goodbye to yet another friend. My logbook note that day says "Sold him a wonderful airplane."

I recently had a note from them. Kyle Wolfe and his wife still have 1932 Charley!

→ **Rule of the Air** ←

Good judgment comes from experience. Unfortunately, the experience usually comes from bad judgment.

There is no right answer to the debate over grass or paved runways. My advice? Be prepared to use both! Let's talk about each, starting with paved runways, on which many pilots train, and fly out of. Some of the advantages include being able to fly year-around, particularly when there are winter snow conditions and the runways are kept plowed.

Other pilots train and fly out of smaller airfields, often with grass runways only. These fields offer the advantages of freedom to depart and arrive quickly, usually with little traffic and no control tower. Lower hangar costs are typical at smaller fields.

Each has its advantages and disadvantages, depending on the pilot's situation. If flying for business purposes, the year-round runways are important. For personal and/or pleasure, grass can be great.

At Poplar Grove Airport (C77) we are fortunate to have a long paved runway (12/30) and two grass runways (17/35 and 9/27). This is a great advantage. We can fly year-around and still have the grass that our taildraggers thrive on.

Small airfields are more numerous and in case of an emergency you should be familiar with them. Next time you are flying, punch "nearest" on your GPS. In the Midwest, over a dozen will often show up within 15 or 20 miles. The runways are shorter and the Unicom radio is different than you are accustomed to on your controlled field.

If you are based on a grass strip, become familiar with the differences at a controlled field. You may need to use one in case of an emergency. You will need to understand Approach Control and Control Tower instructions. (Note: when you turn final on a 10,000-foot concrete runway, remember that the hard surface is not as forgiving as grass, and as I noted in another chapter, when it comes time to flare, the endless concrete made depth perception really difficult.)

REGULATIONS for Operation of AIRCRAFT.

In 1920, the United States War Office purportedly issued a set of rules to regulate the increasing number of aircraft that were taking to the air, many of them unsafely. Some of the rules seem so silly it's hard to believe they're real. Real or not, some are funny! Such as:

2. Never leave the ground with the motor leaking.

6. Pilots should carry hankies in a handy position to wipe off goggles.

9. No machine must taxi faster than a man can walk.

12. If you see another machine near you, get out of the way.

And my favorite:

21. Pilots will not wear spurs while flying.

Thursday
MAY

6

S	M	T	W	T	F
2	3	4	5	6	7
9	10	11	12	13	14
16	17	18	19	20	21
23/30	24/31	25	26	27	28

PHOTO © 2003 PHILIP WALLICK

Fairchild PT-19

Like most World War II aircraft, the PT-19 was not designed with the idea that it would still be flying fifty years later. As a result, some areas, like the wooden wing spars, have to be constantly checked to see that they are sound.

My son Jeff gave me a calendar for Christmas that contained a surprise I didn't find for five months.

Chapter Seven

December 25, 2003
A GIFT — AN INCREDIBLE COINCIDENCE

On Christmas Day, my son Jeff gave me a 2004 aviation calendar full of plane pictures. Remember this calendar; I'll again talk about it later in this chapter.

December 27, 2003
PT-19 IN BURNET, TEXAS ... IS THIS THE ONE?

Ever since Plane Number Six, the Cessna 170, left with its new owner to Minnesota, I had been looking for another PT-19. Sixteen years had passed since my first PT had been sold, and I had never forgotten the huge thrill of open-cockpit flying. There are so few PT-19s still flying, however, that there weren't many on the market. Projects kept popping up, but I wanted one I could immediately fly, not spend years rebuilding.

Suddenly, Fairchild #1941N showed up in *Trade-A-Plane*. I called the owner and arranged to see the plane in Burnet, Texas. It had been fully restored a couple of years earlier, was painted in Army Air Force colors (USAAF) from WWII days, and once again I immediately fell in love with an airplane! I knew this was going to be Plane Number Seven. Burnet is a long way from Poplar Grove, Illinois, and I was running a business, so part of my offer included delivery by the owner. He agreed, as long as he could wait till it was warm enough for a Texas boy to fly north.

April 6, 2004
NUMBER SEVEN ARRIVES IN POPLAR GROVE

April arrived before he felt the weather was good enough, and he still spent three days making the trip. He had to stop for several rain showers, and finally, on a cold day, he landed at our airport, half-frozen! I was just glad it wasn't me.

A fascinating part of aircraft ownership is the ability to trace all previous and present owners through FAA registration history. This plane had 14 owners before me. All were California-based until the Texas owner I bought it from. The first owner took delivery in 1945, just as the war was ending. The primary mission of this model was to train future warbird pilots, and that need had come to an end.

> *A fascinating part of aircraft ownership is the ability to trace all previous and present owners through FAA registration history.*

Every veteran I know always remembers his military dog tag number, and many pilots that I am acquainted with always remember the N numbers of the planes they've owned. The N numbers of my eight airplanes are easy for me to recall, including my Plane Number Three, my first Cessna 210.

As I mentioned in Chapter Two, the 210 was totaled after I sold it, and 732WX is no longer a registered number on FAA records. Maybe this is sort of whimsical, but I like to think that number has been retired like a Hall of Fame football jersey number. That airplane carried us many places and did so safely. I wish all eight were still flying, but, at least, the other seven are.

May 6, 2004
DESTINY?

Now, should there be any doubt I was meant to own this PT-19, remember the calendar I mentioned earlier, the one my son gave me on Christmas Day, 2003? I had been using it on my office desk, and on this date I flipped the page and sat looking at a beautiful photo of a PT-19 in the sky over Los Angeles. Not just any PT-19; MY PT-19! There was no doubt because of the military ID, a large 24 on the fuselage. I had purchased this same plane just two days after I received the calendar as a Christmas gift, but I didn't realize the picture was in the calendar until this May 6 date. Wow!

August 22, 2004
HOW COULD AN "A" PILOT DO THIS?

Remember back when I started grading my landings? I'm looking at the grades in my logbook during this particular summer, and they are all "A"s! Finally, I thought, I had it down pat.

Then, on this flight, I had my nephew Charley Maras with me. Granted, it was a really gusty day, but I created one of my worst landings in a long time. The logbook shows "D-." However, Charley thought it was just great and that I had done it to give him an extra thrill. I explained that it was not planned that way.

Then, two weeks later, I did it again! Landing on 27 facing a late afternoon setting sun, I flared about 10 feet above the runway, thought I had touched down and pulled the power. We dropped like an anvil. My passenger was nice about it. I don't remember him flying with me again, however. Another "D" landing!

After that I ran a streak of "A" landings, and according to the book never had another "D" all the while I had the plane. Why do all bad landings happen when a passenger is aboard?

December 18, 2004 to April 6, 2005
WHAT? NO COLD WEATHER FLIGHTS?

Back in the '80s when I had the first PT-19, I flew it year-round. In those days, our IH dealership also sold snowmobiles (Rupp brand) and our whole family rode them. That cold-weather clothing was perfect for the open cockpit, as you sit down pretty deep in the PT-19, out of the wind.

However, now it's 20 years later and I had decided to park the plane during the cold months. (I had also stopped riding snowmobiles and the motorcycle when it was cold.)

July 4, 2005
ONLY OPEN COCKPITS OFFER THIS
KIND OF A MAGICAL DAY

Another Fourth of July Mount Morris fly-in breakfast was our destination, and my daughter, Linda, was with me. There is nothing quite like an open cockpit on a beautiful day like this. I looked up at the open sky and wondered how I could be so fortunate.

August 10, 2005
THE CLOUD IGNORES ME!

A fleecy cloud at 2,500 feet gave me yet another chance. I'd been trying, unsuccessfully, to tear off a piece of these clouds for years. You fly through the edge of a cloud and look back to see how much damage you did. Again, like each time before, NOTHING! The cloud remains undisturbed, even though a spinning propeller with a large airplane behind it should have shattered the cloud. I've asked other pilots what they think the result of this high-tech experiment would be, and they always believe the cloud would end up a different shape, at least to a small extent. Maybe I'm the only one who enjoys trying this, as futile as it may be. No one else seems to share my curiosity.

June 23, 2005
LOOK UP ... ENJOY THE VIEW!

I'll remember this forever. A friend's son was home on leave from Afghanistan. He was an army helicopter pilot and had never been in an open-cockpit aircraft. We took off and I told him the stick was his. I flew the PT from the front cockpit, and as we climbed, I looked in my mirror and saw that his head was down in the cockpit. The climb was still good. I looked again. All I could see was the top of his head. I suggested he look up at a gorgeous blue-sky day. As I watched in the mirror, he looked up and around, shook his head, and spoke. He said all of his copter flights were at night, and all IFR. He never looked out of the chopper. He said he couldn't believe that he was doing the same in the PT. We both learned something about aviation that day.

September 23, 2006
THUNDERBIRD PILOT IN A PT-19

The Air Force Thunderbird team was scheduled to fly an afternoon program at the Rockford Air Show on this date. A group of us invited them to an early breakfast at our nearby Poplar Grove Airport, and also invited them to fly with us in our classic and vintage planes.

Captain Angela Neff asked to fly with me in the PT-19. As part of that incredible flying team, she was maneuvering the high-tech F-16s in the most precise formations, but she had never flown off a grass runway and had never been in an open-cockpit aircraft.

Captain Neff flew my complex and sophisticated(!) 1941 trainer like a pro, and got a big kick out of flying a plane that has only three basic instruments! We had a great time.

That afternoon, she was back in the F-16 and the Thunderbirds flew their usual great routine at the air show.

April 12, 2008
HERE WE GO AGAIN

A pilot from Texas came up on this date to look at the PT. It seemed time to "return indoors" to a closed-in plane that I could use year-round. Our office now had clients in neighboring states and I again had need for a business aircraft. The PT-19 surely wasn't that.

May 6, 2008
IT GOES BACK TO TEXAS

Three weeks later, the PT was sold. The plane was going back to Texas, where I had found it in 2003. I watched it fly away with its new owner and thought "that's the end of my open-cockpit flying." I had been really fortunate to have owned two great Fairchild PTs through the years and had compiled a large number of unforgettable moments.

March 16, 2016
1941N MOVES ON

According to the FAA Registry, my last PT-19 was purchased by Lone Star Flight Museum. They will open a huge new museum in Galveston during 2017. My "love affair number seven" will look great in its new home!

High Flight

Oh! I have slipped the surly bonds of Earth
And danced the skies on laughter-silvered wings;
Sunward I've climbed, and joined the tumbling mirth
Of sun-split clouds, — and done a hundred things
You have not dreamed of — wheeled and soared and swung
High in the sunlit silence. Hov'ring there,
I've chased the shouting wind along, and flung
My eager craft through footless halls of air ...

Up, up the long, delirious burning blue
I've topped the wind-swept heights with easy grace
Where never lark, nor ever eagle flew —
And, while with silent, lifting mind I've trod
The high untrespassed sanctity of space,
Put out my hand, and touched the face of God.

— *John Gillespie Magee, Jr.*

Scott Wallem, Pro-Case Studio

My eighth plane was my second Cessna 182.

Chapter Eight

May 19, 2008
FROM THE EAST, HERE COMES NUMBER EIGHT

S hortly after my PT-19 left for Texas with its new owner, I started thinking about Plane Number Eight. From 1976-78, I had a Cessna 182 and really liked it, so I decided to find another Skylane.

A well-equipped 182 showed up in Charlottesville, Virginia. The owner had purchased a bigger plane and arranged for the FBO to sell it. The equipment looked good, but it had a high-hour engine and it was priced way too high.

Our engine shop at Poplar Grove Airport, which had been ranked in the top five in the U.S. by business aviation magazines, told me the overhaul would cost over $30,000. With that in mind, our airport owner Steve Thomas, who has advised me with every one of my eight purchases, suggested an offering price.

I told the Charlottesville dealer if he would have the plane flown to Poplar Grove and it passed our mechanic's inspection, I would wire him the price I was offering. The pilot could then fly home on the airlines. If I decided not to buy it, I would pay for half the expense of bringing it to our airport. He agreed.

Every time I have been on the verge of buying an airplane, I hardly sleep the night before. That never happens with cars, just with planes. I guess airplanes affect us differently. It's more than a means to get from home to work, or to the bank and store. A plane promises new adventure.

The PT-19 certainly delivered on that promise, but the open

cockpit limited trips to nearby locations. The Skylane, a closed cockpit, would again permit more distant trips, plus I could fly year-round. I could also return to flying IFR, which I had missed with the PT.

When the 182 arrived, I flew it and really felt at home in it, just like I did with my first 182. The inspection was good, I wired the money and took the pilot to the bus for O'Hare Airport. I had found plane number eight. Lorraine Morris divides her time between her United Airlines 777 cockpits and restoring plane interiors! She earlier renovated my Plane Number Six (170-B) and on my latest 182, she made the interior look new again.

Soon after, we overhauled the engine, installed an engine analyzer, and proximity alert device. I was still grading landings. Because I had so many hours in the previous 182, plus the hours in the 210s, I expected to get "A"s immediately with this plane. Not so! I gave myself "C"s and "B"s till June 16.

June 16, 2008
BACK TO THE 4W RANCH A 14TH TIME!

Beginning in 1995, Bob Kemp, Jerry Pitts and I had flown each year to the 4W Ranch near Newcastle, Wyoming, to spend time with our friends Jean and Bob Harshbarger. In Chapter Five, I wrote about our trips in the 210. According to my Logbook #3, those 1600-mile round trips averaged 10.8 hours.

With the 182, the average trip time was 12.5 hours, which speaks well for the plane. Some years, we had a lot of headwinds outbound. However, even though the 210 had retractable gear and turbocharger, and more horsepower for faster times up to altitude, the travel time between the 210 and the 182 was not greatly different. The economic comparisons between the two suggest that the 182 has an advantage. The cost of the annual on the 182 was substantially less due to fixed gear and naturally aspirated engine. The advantage of the 210

Ready for the 800-mile trip to Wyoming in the 182 with Bob Kemp

in business use was two extra seats, and quicker trips due to the higher speed. Having owned two of each model, I feel the mission of the plane should determine which is better. For long trips and business use, the 210 was wonderful. For personal travel where four seats are sufficient and travel time is less important, the 182 is less expensive to maintain.

June 2009
GOOD ON THE YOKE ... AT AGE NINE!

I met Beckett in California when he was five years old. He was a great kid, and since I had no grandsons, I enjoyed spending time with him and his family. Four years later, they were going to be in Indiana the month of June, so I flew over to Valparaiso and took nine-year-old Beckett up in the 182.

After showing him the altimeter, the airspeed indicator, and bank instruments, I told him to take the yoke and keep the altitude and airspeed steady and the wings level by watching those instruments. I also told him to make very small corrections on the yoke. That's a big assignment for anyone who has never flown, but remarkably, he did just that. Beckett intently studied the gauges and kept the plane absolutely steady on course for several minutes.

I was impressed, and I still am as I've watched Beckett grow. Now 16, he is airborne in a different way. He is practicing for the Junior Olympics snowboarding team. Beckett is still a great kid, AND he's now my step-grandson!

July 27, 2009
BACK TO OSHKOSH

As I did many times in the past, I pitched a tent alongside the plane. There are thousands of planes on Wittman Field every day during

the fly-in, coming and going at all hours. Late-evening and early-morning arrivals and departures can be heard, but somehow, those sounds don't disturb my sleep. They are welcome sounds, music to the ears, at this world-famous event.

The EAA Fly-In provides a great space for pilots to park and camp.

July 25, 2010
A DIFFERENT WAY TO GET TO THE EAA FLY-IN

The weather turned sour on the way to Oshkosh. Low ceilings and wind gusts had incoming traffic backed up all over the area. The Ripon holding pattern was full. Others were told to expect delays of two hours or more.

I chose to land at Dodge County Airport (KUNU). It's a neat, orderly field with friendly staff. In my approximately 30 trips to the EAA Fly-In, I've stopped at Dodge County before when arrivals were backed up. This time local volunteers were offering car rides to Oshkosh. They dropped us off right at the entrance and picked us up again early in the evening. As it turned out, the weather never did improve for air arrivals, so these great folks made it possible to attend.

After many trips to the EAA Fly-In, I suggest this to pilots: If the delays being announced on ATIS are minor, the holding pattern at Ripon works well. However, if major arrival delays are being announced, I've found it better to land nearby and wait for the traffic jam to clear. You'll save enough gas to buy a lot of coffee!

I've always been impressed with the courtesy and cooperation in the aviation community. Everyone is willing to help each other, and the volunteers at Dodge County Airport were one example.

June 5, 2011
LOTS OF CONCRETE. FEW AIRPLANES.

Chanute Air Force Base in Rantoul, Illinois, was established May 21, 1917, as a technical training base. It was decommissioned in 1993 and has since been used for civilian purposes. The non-profit Chanute Air Museum had been on the field for years, with many displays, but closed permanently on November 1, 2015. The Village of Rantoul maintains a civilian airport (KTIP) on the old airbase. When I attended the University of Illinois in the '50s, this military base was very active. It's hard to believe that this base opened almost 100 years ago! During the '70s, my son Jeff spent two weeks there with CAP Encampments. He soloed at 16, and received his pilot's license at age 17.

I had an appointment with a company based at Chanute. As I approached from the north on a long final for 18, the many runways resembled a large, municipal airport. However, the absence of aircraft on the field seemed strange. It reminded me of Ainsworth Regional Airport (KANW), Ainsworth, Nebraska, where we stop to refuel on our Wyoming flights. That too is a decommissioned air base, with lots of runway but very few planes.

Spring, 2012
TIME TO DECIDE

Jeff had purchased our financial planning business, so I no longer needed a business airplane. Most of my friends had flown to breakfast with me many times, but were doing less of that. My daughter, Linda, was living in Los Angeles, too far for this old pilot to fly privately. My youngest child, Steve, was settled in Manhattan, and I had no desire to fly the 182 into the New York area. I started really questioning the need to keep the plane. I knew it was my last one, but had the time come to give it up?

As I approached age 80, it was logical to assume that maintaining a current medical certificate could be a challenge in the future. I was still very healthy, but there was less runway ahead than behind me at this point in life.

I thought about incidents of pilots who had reached advanced ages and kept flying longer than was wise. Yet I was really wondering if I would regret selling the plane after it was gone. Other than my work, flying had been my biggest interest for almost 40 years. The majority of my friends were pilots. I wondered how my friendships would be affected if I no longer flew. I decided to delay the decision for 60 days, and come to a decision by that time to sell or not sell. Then I thought about Chuck Downey.

Fifteen years earlier, on a sunny, summer afternoon in 1997 to be exact, several of us sat in the Poplar Grove flight office watching a mid-'30s Meyers OTW biplane taxi to the gas pumps. FLY NAVY was in large letters on the tail. The pilot wore a long white scarf and a battered leather bomber jacket. Captain Chuck Downey had arrived at Poplar Grove Airport and our lives would never again be the same thanks to this energetic, charismatic, funny man.

> *I was still very healthy, but there was less runway ahead than behind me at this point in life.*

After a long career in aviation, Chuck built a home on Bel-Air Estates with a hangar under his home. Through the years, he flew the Meyers on summer evenings, restored old aircraft in his hangar, and hosted his old Navy buddies. Chuck had been the youngest Naval aviator in WWII, and loved talking about his experiences. He enjoyed his friends and loved talking about his children.

Chuck's decision to quit flying came at age 90. Failing eyesight was a major factor. When he decided to quit flying, we all missed the old Meyers slowly circling the airport in the evenings, but his time had come to quit flying.

Chuck passed away in February 2016, just under a year after he sold the Meyers. We miss him a lot.

July 20, 2012
IT'S TIME

My decision to quit flying came much earlier in my life than it did for Chuck. In May 2012, I added up the hours I had flown during the previous six months. The total was 12.5. I was 78 and I was obviously not flying much. I no longer needed the plane for business purposes, and had flown less during the previous two winters.

In earlier years, I ignored the cold weather and looked for a reason to fly, often just 19 miles to Janesville for breakfast. It was always easy to call a friend at the last minute to go along. As my friends got older, their enthusiasm to fly on a cold day disappeared! I started wondering if my flying days were over.

I decided to put the 182 on the market July 1 — UNLESS I convinced myself in the meantime that I would regret it. After more than 40 years in the air, I wondered. A great friend who had flown with me through the years made a suggestion. Bob Kemp told me to fill the hangar with golf carts, and sell them to pilots in the airpark as well as farmers for use around the farmstead. He thought I would not miss flying as much.

He was right! I sold Cessna 735ZH to Ed Pudlo, a pilot 30 miles away at Galt Airport. In my logbook, there is a notation for this date that says "A good airplane."

I bought some golf carts and never looked back. To this day, I am comfortable with the decision. After 40 years in the air, it was time. Keeping the hangar helped a lot, however. I continue to spend time on the airport with my friends of many years.

Everyone has to face this decision at some point. No one can make it for you. Good luck!

⟶ Rule of the Air ⟵

There are old pilots, and bold pilots, but no old, bold pilots.

Things I've Learned ...

- With every safe landing, we walk away feeling we've scored another victory against gravity.

- Every pilot should try to avoid turbulent flights with passengers who are new to flying. It's a sure way to ruin any enthusiasm they may have for it.

- Make sure your aircraft can handle the weight of your passengers and cargo. Don't be stupid and take chances!

- Before venturing into new situations, talk to experienced pilots and read all you can about proper procedures and the experiences of others. A good example of that is a flatland pilot who plans to fly over mountains for the first time. Another is a large fly-in convention, such as AirVenture.

- Don't assume similar model planes from the same manufacturer have similar features that operate identically, such as the fuel switch on a Cessna 210 vs. a 172 or 182.

- It's wise to seek out crosswind situations to build confidence for the times when you do not have a choice of runway headings.

- Do not fly every flight with the auto-pilot on 100% of the time. You may forget how to use the manual instruments, such as the liquid compass.

FROM	TO	REMARKS, PROCEDURES, MANEUVERS	INSTR APP	NO. LDG	SEL	MEL
Local		B		1		
		w/ Lena. JVl/p		6		
4w + Ret.		w/PITS/kemp.		3		
xal		BT				
il	JVL	1 QT OIL				
	JVL	AA		2		
MT Morris		w/BEnT. Ross C-B 23 AVGIS w/ Lnda walken. BKFST		2	GREAT FLIGHT	

		PAGE TOTAL				
e on this form are true.		AMT. FORWARD				
		TOTAL TO DATE				

DEPARTURE & ARRIVAL		REMARKS, PROCEDURES, MANEUVERS	INSTR APP	NO. LDG
	TO	C - L-		
	JVL	BKFST	ЖΗ	2
	JVL	C - A		2
	WOUK	v		2
		w/ Love + Ants. photos	C - AT	
	JVL-C-77 Lena-577	w/ PITS. BKFST - To Mom House B - B+		2
	JVL-Leonem -PG	Koblosky-Tischent BFST C+A-A+		3
	Emerg	Fen Repair To Tail 5-12 RUSTY DelL back		1
	JVL	BFST 4 2 more RITS A-A		

TYPE OF PILOT

CONDITIONS OF FLIGHT

RAFT CATEGORY & CLASS										
AIRPLANE Single Eng. LAND	AIRPLANE Multieng. LAND	CROSS COUNTRY	DAY	NIGHT	ACTUAL Instrument	AIRCRAFT (HOODED)	SYNTHETIC TRAINER	DUAL RECEIVED	PILOT IN COMMAND	
									3	2
3:2		3:2	3:2						7	6
7:6		7:6	7:6						1	4
1:4		1:4	1:4						2	6
2:6		2:6	2:6						0	6
:6			0:6						5	6
5:6		5:6	5:6						0	6
:6			0:6							
21:6		20:4	21:6	0:0		0:0		0:0	21	
		22:0	1:2		3:2			26:5		

Part Two

The Standard
**PILOT
LOGBOOK**

Special Adventures

Flying a Blimp

Flying a Glider

Building a Museum

and

Other Stuff

*Neil Armstrong said that being in a glider is the closest
you can come to being a bird. I agree.*

Chapter Nine

September 15, 1985
MY FIRST GLIDER FLIGHT

The Huntley Glider Club invited our Vintage Aero Club to exchange rides. We would offer them rides in our vintage and antique planes, and they in turn would take us up in their dual gliders. I gave two glider pilots rides in my Fairchild PT-19, and then my turn came in the glider.

What a strange feeling it was to sit in that cockpit! It appeared to have just completed a wheels-up landing, as I could reach out and touch the grass. When the pilot in command closed the cockpit, I realized I had never been in such a small space. We started the tow, and suddenly the loud snap indicated the line had separated from the Bird Dog towing us. That was another new sensation for me.

Again, we started the tow, and this time we were airborne quickly. The silence was deafening! I had watched glider flights on videos, but never realized everything would be so quiet. The freedom from engine sound reminded me so much of sailboating. Having nature for your only power is quite humbling.

The next challenge was to keep the glider behind the tow plane. Aileron use created too severe a correction and I couldn't stop the pendulum halfway. Rudder steer, like small corrections on an ILS approach, seemed to work best.

We arrived at altitude, 3,000 feet, and when I pulled the tow release it felt like I had unplugged the horizon, because it disappeared, as did the tow plane. What I had done was to unconsciously pull back the stick to avoid dropping, so up went the nose!

The following ten minutes of keeping this sensitive, long-winged sparrow on a level keel was another once-in-a-lifetime experience. The approach to land was too high and fast, until we dropped the speed brakes. That felt like we had thrown out an anchor. Both speed and altitude evaporated, and we were skate-boarding along the runway till there was a sudden stop. Where's the rollout? There wasn't one.

> *Having nature for your only power is quite humbling.*

My reaction to the landing was sheer wonder. This fantastic, graceful machine when airborne suddenly became awkward. After stopping, it lies there as if broken, with one wing touching the ground.

This is a much different aspect of aviation, and I now understand why it is so exhilarating.

→ Rule of the Air ←

Gravity is not just an idea. It's a law.
And it is not subject to appeal.

The Last Bouquet

I've flown 'em all from then till now
The big ones and the small,
I've looped and zoomed and dove and spun
And climbed 'em to a stall.
I've flown them into wind and storm,
Through thunder clouds and rain
And thrilled the folks who watched me roll
My wheels along their train.

I've chased the steers across the range,
The geese from off the bay.
I've flown between the Princeton towers
When Harvard came to play,
I've clipped the wires from public poles
The blossoms from the trees
And scared my best friends half to death
With stunts far worse than these.

The rules and codes and zones they form
Are not for such as I,
Who like the great wild eagles fling
My challenge to the sky,
A bold free spirit charging fierce
Across the fallow land ...
And don't you like these nice white flowers
I'm holding in my hand?

— *Gill Rob Wilson, founder of the Civil Air Patrol*

*Remember when cameras used film? Fuji used a blimp to pro-
mote its brand and brought it to Oshkosh in 1997.*

Chapter Ten

August 3, 1997
WE FLY THE FUJI BLIMP

The EAA Convention was in full swing in Oshkosh when the late Bob Collins of WGN Radio in Chicago and I were invited to fly in the Fuji Blimp. My good friend Bill Bowden from Belvidere was one of the Fuji pilots, and suggested we join them for a flight over the convention grounds.

It's a huge airship — it stands as tall as a six-story building and is 50 feet in diameter. We climbed into the cabin, which had seats for eight passengers and two crew members. After we were untethered, we rose to 1000 feet and Bob and I took turns behind the yoke. What an incredible, different kind of flight this was! The craft is nearly 200 feet in length. A long ribbon hangs from the nose, well ahead and above the cockpit. The ribbon indicates the direction of drift and the pilot compensates with the rudder. This is a new definition of "high" tech.

It reminded me of a giant banana being pushed around the sky by the wind. We were in a mild breeze from the west, yet it took full deflection of the yoke — both ways — to maintain a circular heading over the convention area. I quickly understood why the two pilots change as PIC every 15 or 20 minutes, as your shoulders really get a workout. Fatigue came fast in my case.

Engine noise, barely audible to people on the ground, was very high in the cockpit. It was a hot day, so all of the windows were open, which is another big difference from an airplane. Wind entering the

Bob Collins getting a workout at the
Fuji Blimp controls

cockpit wasn't an issue because we were only traveling five mph or so. The blimp has a top speed of about 35 mph.

As our host pilots steered the blimp back to land, the nose-down attitude felt strange, as if we were going to nose into the ground. However, with reverse props, we were moving slowly, and several of the 18-member ground crew grabbed our trailing lines and tied us into a secure position.

Even though blimps are big and slow, safe landings aren't guaranteed. Less than a year after our flight in Oshkosh, the Fuji Blimp was landing at the Birmingham, Alabama, airport. With about 10 feet to go, a gust of wind caught the blimp and blew it against a fence. According to a report by the Associated Press, the pilot pulled a ripcord to quickly deflate the bag, which contained 233,000 cubic feet of helium. The two pilots and two passengers were not injured, but that was a landing they'll likely never forget.

There are many ways to fly. This was certainly an unusual one, and great for sight-seeing at a slow pace. And what a short-field landing it was!

One of the blimp's two engines, with a nice view of the EAA grounds

Two fixed-wing pilots enjoying their ride in a giant flying banana

When I took my turn at the yoke, it handled unlike any aircraft I had flown, and it was exhausting, too!

*The control panel of my third love, a
Cessna T-210 Centurion. Should I take it, or
Braniff, to San Antonio?*

Chapter Eleven

MAY 12, 1982

TO SAN ANTONIO ... PRIVATE OR COMMERCIAL?

An upcoming San Antonio business appointment gave me the option to either fly my Plane Number Three (Cessna T-210), or go commercial.

Running the numbers, I estimated the flight time with the 210 from Poplar Grove, Illinois, to San Antonio would be about six hours one way. Flying commercial would mean a drive to O'Hare, a flight to Dallas, and a connecting flight to San Antonio; total time about four hours. A cost comparison indicated fuel alone for the 210 would cost $410. The round-trip airline ticket would be $270. Braniff was the best choice, regarding schedule and price. Also, the commercial ride would give me time to prepare for the meeting. So, the decision to fly commercial seemed the right one.

On the departure day, I left home about 5:45 a.m. to drive to O'Hare. I had two large audio/visual cases which Braniff check-in folks wanted to charge extra for, but finally agreed there would be no fee. (Can you imagine that happening these days?)

We loaded at 8 a.m. I ended up in the center of a five-abreast row. I am 6' 1" and always try for an aisle seat, but on this DC-10 flight I couldn't get that. This moment became the first of many when I wondered if I should have flown myself. The left seat in the 210 is like an easy chair.

We pushed back from the ramp at 8:15, taxied to the runway and were told that an exit door needed fixing. We returned to the ramp for repairs, and finally departed sometime after 9 a.m. It looked like I would miss my Braniff connecting flight out of Dallas to San Antonio. Once again, I wished I had voted to fly the 210. If I had left the house that morning at the same time, 5:45 and driven to my hangar, I would have been in the air with the 210 by 6:30. Allowing time for a fuel stop, I would have landed in San Antonio by 1 p.m.

Because this was a breakfast flight, I hadn't eaten earlier. I should have. It was now 10:45 a.m. and breakfast was just being served. At 11 a.m., a two-year old started crying near me, and kept it up for eight minutes. I gave up trying to work, and couldn't help but think of the peaceful cockpit of the 210.

Our DC-10 captain must have stayed on afterburner all the way, because he made up all but 20 minutes of the lost time. I told the cabin attendant my problem regarding the connecting flight, so she moved me up front near the exit. I got on the flight to San Antonio with minutes to spare. But our clearance was held up, and we finally landed in San Antonio at 1:45 p.m., almost an hour later than I would have with the 210.

Two close friends had arrived before me, International Harvester executive Stan Lancaster and Orion Samuelson of WGN. The three of us presented a convention program together the next morning. That afternoon, Orion was flying back to Chicago on American, while Stan was on my Braniff flight. When Stan and I got to the airport to catch the 3 p.m. flight to Dallas, we were told the flight would be delayed due to a thunderstorm near Dallas.

We finally boarded at 5 p.m. Suddenly, a TV crew came on

board to film and interview the flight crew. Seems that Braniff had declared bankruptcy moments before and was closing down all operations that evening.

The plane continued to sit at the gate, gradually filling with Dallas-based flight crews and personnel who had been told to get back to Dallas before midnight on a Braniff flight or travel at their own expense. Some were crying as they boarded.

We finally got in the air to Dallas and the cabin attendants opened the bar service without charging for drinks. Passengers were consoling Braniff employees, and one passenger went down the aisle with his hat, asking everyone to donate. The hat was overflowing before he finished, and the money was split among the cabin attendants, as this was their last day to work.

To make matters worse, we flew into the storm that had held us on the ground earlier. It was raining. The air was bumpy. Braniff employees, stunned at their plight, were crying. It was really a mess.

> It was raining. The air was bumpy. The Braniff employees, stunned at their plight, were crying. It was really a mess.

As we started descending, a cabin attendant announced on the PA system that our flight was beginning a VERY FINAL APPROACH to DFW airport.

As we disembarked, a passenger joked about who would pay if luggage is lost. We entered the Braniff Terminal, which was locked up and closed. A security officer directed us to the baggage area where everything was chaos. Passengers with Braniff tickets for connecting flights, like Stan and me, knew that Braniff wouldn't be flying us any further, and that we were on our own. We immediately went to other airline counters but they had already been invaded by earlier arrivals. Every flight out of Dallas to Chicago was filled for the night. It was also obvious that no other airlines would be honoring our Braniff tickets, so that investment was lost.

A young army private had been sitting between Stan and me on the flight we had just been on. He was en route home to Chicago on a ticket his mother had sent him. He was about 18, had only $20 cash, and was really scared about getting home. We told him to stick with us and assured him we would get him home.

Before that, though, we needed to find a place to spend the night. Thousands of other people who were stranded by Braniff were in the same boat, so it took quite a while before we finally found motel rooms a long way from the airport. We took our Army private with us and he slept on a roll-away in my room. Late the next morning, the three of us boarded American and flew to Chicago.

We said goodbye to our private at O'Hare and he promised to repay us. One week later, Stan had a check from the boy's mother for the cost of the ticket.

After I added up the cost of the motel room, two long taxi rides, and the American ticket to Chicago, as well as a day lost from work, you can understand that the 210 flight would have been a bargain!

⟶ Rule of the Air ⟵

The three most useless things to a pilot are the altitude above you, runway behind you, and a tenth of a second ago.

If you think being a pilot is tough,
try being a pilot's wife.
— Anonymous (but probably a pilot's wife)

On left base for Runway 12 at C77, Poplar Grove Airport

Chapter Twelve

THE GREAT AVIATION TRIO - PHASE ONE
1972
AN AIRPORT GROWS IN A CORNFIELD

Dick Thomas was dairying near Belvidere, Illinois. Bob Rice was President of the Belvidere Bank. The author (that's me) was the IH farm equipment dealer in town. We met at the Huddle Restaurant every Monday at 10 a.m. to drink coffee and settle the problems of the world.

Dick was mowing a runway in his hayfield, where he and his sons Steve and Billy were having a great time flying a Piper Cub. One Monday morning at the Huddle, Dick commented about building an airport. Wow! This was a long way from discussing the world's problems.

Over the next few weeks, he talked about it more. Bob Rice said his bank would help with the financing. My son Jeff was a member of Rockford's CAP squadron and was really excited about flying, and I told Dick I would like to learn.

The Huddle was coffee crossroads for a lot of the local businessmen, and some of them were stopping at our table to tell Dick they, too, would like to learn to fly. Bob Lear, Jack Wolf, Howard Miller, Jerry Marrs, Doc Carlyle, and George Fleming were just some of them.

It all happened fast! After Dick and his partners started Belvidere Airport (C77) on a dairy farm between Belvidere and Poplar Grove, the entire community got excited. Every one of the previously named wannabe pilots not only learned to fly, but bought planes and based them at our new airport. I did the same.

In the years that followed, the Belvidere Airport grew into a home away from home for all of us that had learned to fly. New students were learning every day. I bought my first plane, a Cessna 172. Dick Thomas started restoring a vintage Waco UPF7, and I would stop on the way home from work to watch his progress. On the weekends, the airport was a beehive of activity. It also became home for a variety of vintage planes, including Stearman, Waco, Beechcraft, Fairchild and a lot more. There was the feeling of an airfield from the '30s, yet completely modern in facilities and service. It still has that same great atmosphere.

Dick Thomas died in 1994. Bob Rice had passed away earlier. I miss that Monday morning coffee at the Huddle with these two great friends. Following Dick's death, Steve and Tina Thomas, Dick's son and daughter-in-law, bought the airport. In order to build an adjacent air-

The Poplar Grove Airport, Bel-Air Estates, and Vintage Wings and Wheels Museum

park, they annexed the field to the community of Poplar Grove, and the name became Poplar Grove Airport. Bel-Air Estates is home to over a hundred families with hangars that have access to the runways. More pilots live in 48 on-site condos. A lot of airline personnel live here.

Poplar Grove is now home to over 400 planes. The grass is always mowed, the snow is always plowed. A formation of Stearmans will fly over, and soon after a formation of RVs that were built by their owners, and all of them call C77 home! At times like this, it's obvious that this is a special place. The State of Illinois agrees, because in 2010, it named our field "Airport of the Year." This was the second time our airport received this award. The first was in 1997.

Most pilots consider a good maintenance department a high priority when they are looking for a home base. I think of the 30 years that Dave Noe and his great mechanics took care of my eight airplanes. I know I could not have had better service anywhere.

Through the years, our airport has held a huge fly-in breakfast on the third Sunday of August. Some years, over 2,000 have been fed by a great group, the Poplar Grove Lions Club. I hope you will come!

Lastly, I have often chuckled through the years when I hear a strange pilot on Unicom, asking for POP-U-LAR Grove weather and wind. Upon second thought, I realize that all of us local folks do indeed feel this is a popular place! And, as owner Steve Thomas told writer Jon McGinty in the Autumn 2015 *Northwest Quarterly*, "This is a positive place. It's a place where people can get away from the day-to-day grind, experience the freedom of flight, and be around airplane people. We like it here."

Photo: Jon McGinty

Tina and Steve Thomas, (with Charlie and Carson). Without them, and the vision they shared with Steve's dad, Dick, none of what we have at Poplar Grove Airport would be possible.

THE GREAT AVIATION TRIO - PHASE TWO

August 18, 1996
BUILD AN "OLD PLANE" MUSEUM ... ARE WE NUTS?

Several of us were sitting under a Waco wing. It was our 24th annual Airport Fly-in Breakfast. Steve Thomas threw out this idea: "Let's build a museum for old planes."

Sounded like a lot of work. Even though our airfield had become home for a lot of vintage and classic aircraft, a project like this sounded like money. LOTS OF MONEY. So we all finished our breakfast and went our separate ways. Interesting idea, though.

December 12, 1996
SHOULD WE GO AHEAD WITH THIS?

Sitting in my office were Steve and Tina Thomas, Dick and Bobbie Wagner, Pat Packard and me. Lots of ideas flew around the room. No shy voices here! What a challenge this would be, creating a museum. Steve and Tina were well along in building a first-class private airport, with emphasis on old planes. Dick and Bobbie were operating Wag-Aero, their large aviation parts house. Pat Packard was winding up 14 years at EAA headquarters in Oshkosh, designing the interior of its new museum. My interest came from a tour of the Museum of Flight in Santa Monica, California, the prior year. What a place! I learned at this meeting that Pat Packard had also done interior design for that museum.

My wife, Joan, was office manager at our financial planning practice, and our son Jeff had just resigned from Sundstrand Corporation to join us, so I felt I could devote some time to this project. Little did I know that it would require endless hours for many years!

We met again in January and decided to charge ahead with plans for a museum, focusing on aircraft during the period from 1903 to 1938. We each made an initial contribution to start the procedure for a not-for-profit organization.

Also, we are now actively soliciting donations, to support the cost of printing, mailing etc. for the coming fund-raising events. The minor costs to date have been shared by the Advisors. Your financial help will greatly influence the success of the Museum. Your donations are tax deductible.

The goal is to build the headquarters building pictured below during 1998. With your help, it will happen!

Paul S. Wallem

A sketch of the proposed museum used during fund-raising

Spring 1997
UP AND RUNNING!

Steve Thomas donated use of an office in the engine shop. Amcore Bank donated all the furniture we needed. Jerry Pitts and I hauled two truckloads of furniture. We re-carpeted, painted the walls, and opened with Nancy Pearse being our first employee as office manager. Curt Tobin answered our legal questions, without charge. We started designing buildings and planning fund-raising activities.

November 25, 1997
IT'S OFFICIAL

The IRS notified us that we had been granted not-for-profit status with the classification listed as:

POPLAR GROVE AVIATION EDUCATION ASSOCIATION, dba
POPLAR GROVE VINTAGE WINGS AND WHEELS MUSEUM.

May 9, 1998
FUND-RAISER PAYS OFF BIG-TIME!

Following a huge effort by volunteers, this first of many fund-raising banquets brought in over $53,000 in cash and pledges. Our fledgling museum finally had a bank account! The airport let us use its large maintenance shop for this and many future events.

May 8, 1999
WHERE CAN WE SEAT ALL OF THEM?

Here we were with 508 reservations for this second banquet! Sorta looks like people have heard about our new museum! Anyway, with the help of dozens of volunteers, we stuffed more tables into the hangar, and a great evening produced over $30,000 in donations.

As with the 1998 banquet, Orion Samuelson and Bob Collins of WGN Radio in Chicago gave us a lot of free advertising and contributed their own dollars as well. While Bob is no longer with us, Orion continues to support the museum in many ways: as advisor, event MC and donor. It would be impossible to measure his input to our success through the years, and many out-of-town visitors have come in response to his radio comments.

Summer 1999
ARE WE NUTS ... AGAIN?

Waukesha Airport Authority donated its inactive 1938 Lannon Stone hangar to us. We were thrilled and grateful, but there was one very large problem. Waukesha is about 80 miles from our airport!

Dennis Harms was museum president at that time, and put in endless hours along with others helping to acquire this building.

Undaunted, we hired Rockford Blacktop to dismantle the hangar, stone by stone, beam by beam, and truck the pieces to Poplar Grove. What a job. In 2000, we rebuilt it and it became our main building. Dennis Blunt created a beautiful diorama of the building, which we used for fund-raising for several years.

OPENING DAY 2003

At this point I'm going to fast-forward four years, and in that period of time, dozens of volunteers had raised money, built buildings, conducted youth aviation programs and much more. Here are examples of some of their efforts:

- Annual fund-raising banquets 1998-2007
- $1000 pledge drive 1998 with 53 pledges
- "Pathway to the Past" paving bricks were sold at $100.
- A 1999 museum calendar was designed. 700 were sold at $50.

During this same period, the following buildings were obtained and erected:

- 1928 Springfield Hangar
- 1938 Waukesha Hangar
- 1927 Hamilton T-Hangar
- 1924 Sunoco Gas Station
- 1927 Slim's Garage

June 12, 2003
GRAND OPENING! BUT IT'S POURING DOWN RAIN

We hadn't poured a sidewalk yet and the museum entrance was mud! Butch Rafferty and Eric Wilkins laid 4' x 8' plywood for a temporary sidewalk, and the banquet was another great success.

At all these banquets, the period costumes worn by many volunteers added to the evening. We never knew what Lorraine Morris, Tina Thomas, Butch Rafferty and other volunteers would be wearing those nights, and guests loved it! More about Butch: The museum would not be what it is today without the many contributions of work and donations from him and Betsy.

SINCE 2003

Hundreds of volunteers have conducted events such as family fly-days, ag-days, classic car shows, wheels shows (including horse-drawn vehicles, tractors, cars and planes), L-Bird fly-ins, wine tasting parties and murder mystery dinners. Eric Wilkins was the first museum coordinator, Dave Stadt took over from him. Next came Kip Kirkland, and now Judi Zangs is general manager. For many years before she joined the staff, Judi was a volunteer, including editing the museum newsletter. She is currently assisted by Trudi Konopka and Mike Fredericksen.

Past presidents have been Paul Wallem, Dennis Harms, Kendra Helvey, Butch Rafferty and Peggy Fry. Ken Starzyk serves presently, and has served several terms. Cindy Starzyk is always there helping. Our original gift shop manager and volunteer coordinator was Patricia Cox. From

Max Armstrong and Orion Samuelson with their refurbished Farmalls
outside the Vintage Wings and Wheels Museum

the early days, Nick Scheurer created the library, with much help from
Cheryl Falardeau. Ken Morris served as treasurer during a particularly
busy period from 1999-2001.

September 4, 2010
A SHOW FULL OF WHEELS

This was first of a series of events featuring all kinds of wheels,
including carriages, tractors, cars airplanes, and even a horse-drawn
hearse. On a cold, very windy day a good crowd still came. Ken and
Lorraine Morris made trophies for the best displays.

For the following wheels show in 2011, we added classic farm
tractors. Max Armstrong of WGN had his vintage "560" hauled from
downstate for our show, along with the restored Farmall "F-20" that Orion
grew up on. Max interviewed many of our tractor owners that day, for airing
later on WGN and their weekly TV show, "This Week in Agribusiness."

May 2012
WHY IS ELREY JEPPESEN STANDING OUT FRONT?

When you walk into the Denver International Airport terminal you see an 18-foot bronze statue of aviation pioneer Elrey Jeppesen. Only a couple of other replicas of this famous aviator existed until Jack and Peggy Wolf donated the funds to put a statue identical to Denver's at our front door. Visitors stop from far and wide to see the magnificent statue of Elrey and tour our museum.

John Larson spent a lot of time preparing a foundation for our statue. A group of volunteers spent months raising money for the grounds around Elrey. Peggy Fry organized a great dedication event.

Also in 2012, plans were finalized to build a restoration hangar shared by our museum and EAA Chapter 1414. It's now a beautiful new building with restoration projects underway at both ends.

2016
GROWTH CONTINUES, VISITORS KEEP COMING

Vintage Wings and Wheels Museum has hosted thousands of visitors since its beginning. Hundreds of volunteers had given their time and money to provide a unique Museum. The generosity of local business sponsors has been overwhelming through the years. It's obvious that this museum would be much smaller, and with far fewer facilities and events, without the support of local businesses.

It's great fun to meet pilots stopping en route to or from EAA AirVenture. We hope you will stop in, too.

THE GREAT AVIATION TRIO - PHASE THREE
2005
THE START OF SOMETHING BIG

Let's look back. In 1972, Dick Thomas started the Belvidere

Aviation pioneer Elrey Jeppesen and sculptor George Lundeen flank Mr. Jeppesen's statue. We commissioned Lundeen to sculpt a copy of the original statue that now stands outside the Vintage Wings and Wheels Museum.

Airport. In 1996, a group of four founders started Vintage Wings and Wheels Museum. The third part of this great trilogy came about in 2005.

Frank Herdzina and Walt Schultz thought it was time to have an EAA chapter on our airport. Frank said he would do the paperwork, but after that he wanted to back away and work on his plane projects: a 1930 Bird and a 1934 F2 Cub. But Frank went further by lining up 18 individuals who would consider being directors. A meeting was scheduled.

(AUTHOR'S NOTE: I couldn't help but chuckle when Frank said he was going to "back away." He's still trying to "back away.")

February 5, 2005
A NEW CHAPTER IS BORN

The first meeting of the Poplar Grove EAA Chapter was in the airport's maintenance shop, thanks to Steve and Tina Thomas, and Dave Noe and his crew who cleared the shop and cleaned it up for the group. Of 73 in attendance, 42 were already paid members. The group heard that the EAA had approved the chapter, and lifetime EAA member John Larson, one of the first to sign up for the new chapter, commented that there was a lot of enthusiasm at this first get-together.

March 1, 2005
WE'RE OFFICIAL!

EAA President Tom Poberezny signed the charter for Chapter 1414 on this date. Also signing were 18 charter members:

Sam Helsper (first president), Tom Barnes, Frank Herdzina, Alexander Von Bosse, Jeannie Hill, Sam Kelso, Ken Kresmery, Don Alesi, Dan Helsper, John Larson, Steve Langdon, Kerry Peters, Diana Ingram, Tina Thomas, Don Pfeiffer, Lee Hilbert, Robert Fry, Bill Turner

Tom Barnes became the second president, and Steve Langdon became the third. The chapter used Frank's big box hangar as headquarters for years. Tables and chairs were borrowed, along with other equipment, to begin Sunday breakfasts, which continue to this day.

Lee Hilbert succeeded Steve Langdon and became the longest-serving president, leading the chapter until 2014. Membership continued to grow, as did the pancake breakfasts and other activities. Alex Von Bosse put out a newsletter to keep everyone informed, and it was recognized one year by EAA as the outstanding chapter newsletter.

Glenda May took over that task for many years.

Lee wanted 1414 to be "everybody's chapter, including kids." In 2007, Lee felt the EAA Young Eagles Program should become a major effort for the chapter. An enthusiastic new member, Ed Meyers, became the Young Eagles Coordinator. Ed brought new energy to the project, posting signs all over the Rockford area, encouraging parents to bring kids to Sunday breakfasts and get a free plane ride. The Young Eagles program grew rapidly and is still going strong.

2011

As Chapter 1414 continued to thrive, it was time to consider obtaining its own home base. Steve Thomas had suggested to Museum President Butch Rafferty that the museum and the EAA chapter should consider collaborating on a new building. Frank Herdzina, Lee Hilbert and Butch began discussing the idea. The end result was a new building to house the museum's restoration projects in one half, and the EAA chapter would lease the other half where it would have a kitchen for the pancake breakfasts, and space for all its other activities

Many people spent a great deal of time to make this new space happen for both the museum and the EAA. Butch Rafferty headed up the museum side. Frank, and Wally Falardeau virtually lived in the EAA hangar for many months creating a new home for Chapter 1414. Craig Day, Don Perry and others also helped find special deals on carpet, tile, AC, and other necessities came from trade unions, with a lot of help from Don.

May 2013
GRAND OPENING

Jeff Skiles, known throughout the aviation world as well as EAA, was the guest speaker at the opening of Chapter 1414's headquarters. Since then, the chapter has made great use of its new build-

Jeff Skiles (EAA) signed a beautiful wooden plaque commemorating the opening of the Poplar Grove EAA chapter's hangar.

ing. A pledge drive was highly successful to offset costs of the new building. And the pancake breakfasts continue to net enough to support the chapter's operational costs.

2014

Ed Meyers became president, and his enthusiasm continues to help the chapter grow and prosper. Huge volunteer efforts by members, which now number over 100, include the many hours spent by Dean May managing the Sunday breakfasts. Don Perry, Steve Langdon, Lee Hilbert, Bernie McLean, Adolph Svec, Chuck Pazdzioch and many others have made Chapter 1414 an organization to be proud of.

Jon McGinty

*The Poplar Grove EAA pancake breakfasts
are an opportunity for generations to
come together and enjoy aviation.*

Visitors from across the country are impressed by our Great Aviation Trio:

Poplar Grove Airport (1972)
Poplar Grove Vintage Wings and Wheels Museum (1996)
EAA Chapter 1414 (2005)

It's a great lineup!

September 17, 1983
Orion, with me on his right, sees 6184C for the first time.

Chapter Thirteen

"AIR ORION" ... A TRUE BUSINESS AIRPLANE

"Air Orion," aka 6184C, is a Cessna T-210 Centurion that just might hold a world record, all things considered! As a business aircraft, the story behind this airplane is incredible.

> Same owner: 33 years
> Same mission: 33 years
> Trip cancellations for mechanical reasons: 3
> Tach hours during 33 years: 5000-plus
> Damage history: none
> Same pilots: 28 years
> Average annual use: 160 hours

The outstanding reliability of this plane, and the business benefits to its owner, are a story in itself.

Orion Samuelson and I bought 84C on September 12, 1983. It was a 1980 model with slightly over 200 hours on the tach. Orion has been the best-known voice on WGN Radio Chicago since 1960, and through the years, he has traveled weekly to speaking engagements in the agricultural industry throughout the Midwest. Orion typically drove to many events, sometimes several in one week, and often returned home late at night after his speech so he could be back on the radio early the next morning. After falling asleep at the wheel and nearly crashing one night in Pontiac, Illinois, he agreed that flying would be a better way to go. So he and I bought this plane together. We had a great partnership. His schedule allowed him to plan trips well in advance, and my use of the plane at our IH dealership was flexible.

Retired U.S. Air Force Major Bob Harshbarger was instructing at our airport, Poplar Grove, Illinois (C77), and Orion hired him to do the flying. Orion has never chosen to become a licensed pilot. His intense commitment to work left little time to become proficient in the air, but his real concern was he would take too many weather chances if he had a speaking commitment on the other side of a line of thunderstorms and he "just had to be there." Orion has always said, "If my pilots don't want to fly in certain weather conditions, neither do I."

When I sold my business in 1986 and no longer had use for a business airplane, Orion became sole owner. In 1988, Bob Harshbarger moved to Wyoming and Mike Hudgins took over the piloting until he, too, moved elsewhere in 1996. United Airlines Second Officer Jerry Lagerloef signed on, and has been flying 84C for Orion ever since. When Jerry moved up to captain at United, his schedule became tighter, and Phill Wolfe, with American Airlines, joined Jerry in 1998 to share the flying. Both are still piloting 84C.

WGN listeners are familiar with the name "Air Orion," as it has been mentioned on the air many times as various hosts and Orion talked about his travels. The credit for the name goes to Bob Collins. The credit for booking Orion's speeches goes to his wife, Gloria. She manages his speaking schedule and the airplane makes her job easier. She can schedule Air Orion instead of an airline when a speaking location favors community airports. (I should add that as a former regional manager for the Peninsula Hotel group, and a former sales manager at The Ritz in London, Gloria is over-qualified for this job.)

This extremely reliable business aircraft has been a workhorse that has carried Orion to his speaking engagements throughout the

Air Orion over familiar territory: Midwest farmland

Midwest these past 33 years, with virtually no mechanical cancellations. There was one hair-raising incident that Orion wrote about in his book, *You Can't Dream Big Enough,* where the engine locked up late one night and an emergency landing was made at the Galt airport (10C) in McHenry County, Illinois. Owner Arthur Galt built the strip in a corn field, and fortunately for Orion, decided to leave the runway lights on all night, just in case.

Orion speaks to agricultural audiences in small communities, and thanks to Air Orion, he can fly into local airports. Many of his destinations are not near commercial airports with airline service.

The value of a local community airport is significant. Without it, individuals and business representatives would find it much more difficult to attend local functions and have access to local businesses. Every community benefits when they support a local airfield.

One paint job, three engines and 5000 hours later, 84C is the same reliable, fast business plane that it has always been. I recently asked pilots Jerry and Phill if they ever wished they were flying a twin instead. Their answer was "no." The Midwest is flat terrain, and no mountains are involved in any of their trips.

Phill and Jerry also stated that even though Orion chose not to get a license, he has spent considerable time at the controls, and they believe he could successfully put the plane on the ground in the event of pilot sickness.

84C has been a remarkable business aircraft, with a blue-ribbon history of reliable performance. Numerous avionics upgrades have been installed to keep the equipment current, and 84C shows no signs of quitting. Nor, I should add, does Orion; 84C is not for sale!

An Air Orion business card, circa 1992
Courtesy: Mike Hudgins

———➤ Rule of the Air ⬅———
Weather forecasts are horoscopes with numbers.

Time spent flying is not deducted from one's lifespan.
Old pilots never die ... they just go on to a new plane.
— Anonymous

Courtesy: EAA Oshkosh

The arrow points to the pilot's target at AirVenture, one of three large dots painted on the runway for simultaneous landings.

Chapter Fourteen

SO YOU'RE FLYING TO AIRVENTURE!

This is the closest thing to a carrier landing for a private pilot. It's really a spectacular event. There's nothing like it in all of aviation. I've attended over two dozen times, and it's always exciting.

For many years the official name of the event was the EAA Annual Convention and Fly-In. In 1998, the name was changed to AirVenture Oshkosh, but many of the regulars and old-timers still refer to it as the EAA, Oshkosh Airshow or just Oshkosh. Whatever you want to call it, I call it fun! 500,000 pilots and friends roam around thousands of parked planes, meet new friends, eat good food and enjoy what Wilbur and Orville started.

Here's the best advice I can give you regarding AirVenture: If you are flying in, BRIEF YOUR PASSENGERS! They will not be accustomed to seeing other planes very close to them. It can be incredibly scary if you haven't prepared them. I took my wife, Joan, and son, Steve, once and I didn't think to explain to her that planes might be very close ahead, behind and alongside some of the time. Joan found it very unnerving. Steve sat in the back seat laughing because he loved it!

Reassure your passengers that 50 FAA controllers work this convention, and they do an amazing job. Through all these years since the early '70s, there has never been a collision in the air.

I've always started planning the trip early. You might want to download the information several days ahead of departure. If it's your first time, read all of it!

Some days, the tower will direct over 3,000 flights. Controllers love this assignment and volunteer for it. They are allowed only seven assignments to the Fly-In, so that other controllers can get in on the fun.

There are two runways on Wittman Field, a north-south 18/36 and an east-west 9/27. Large painted dots on the runway are used to work landings simultaneously. It's not unusual for 10 or more landings and departures to occur every minute — one every six seconds? Wow!

Wittman Field controllers in the tower work closely with controllers located at Ripon and Fisk, which are control points. I've always tuned in ATIS early, so I can digest that information ahead of arrival at Ripon. At Ripon it's time to line up with the railroad tracks to Fisk. (Nothing new about this system, it's been in place for over 40 years!)

Here's a preview of what you'll hear as you near Fisk. This is a sample of the <u>one-way</u> conversation from controllers at Fisk. (THEY do ALL the talking, you just listen.)

Fisk Controller: You need to look out your window and line up over the tracks from Ripon ... Directly over the tracks at 1800 feet and 90 knots ... Cessna 150 approaching Fisk rock your wings. Keep your speed up 50, monitor tower 118.5 ... Another 150 approaching Fisk, rock your wings. Good. Champ approaching Fisk, rock your wings ... now make right turn Champ, and fly eastbound. Plan left traffic for 36, monitor 126.6 ... low wing directly over Fisk rock your wings, follow the tracks monitor 118.5 ... Cessna high-wing at Fisk, rock your wings ... Centurion, rock your wings ... you should be at 1800 feet. Follow the tracks for runway 9 monitor

*118.5 ... Low-wing approaching Fisk, rock your wings ...
follow the tracks monitor 118.5.*

That was verbatim from an actual recording. If you were to read it at a normal rate, it would probably take 45 seconds. But I want to prepare you for your arrival at Fisk, and when I timed this actual conversation, it was only 28 seconds! So be ready for rapid-fire instructions, and be aware that the controllers are using binoculars to pick out each plane they are instructing. BE READY TO LISTEN FAST!

Now, maybe you've been given "118.5." Here's a small sample of what you will hear from that frequency at the tower:

Centurion over the shoreline on a short final for 27 land, on the orange dot. Welcome to Oshkosh. RV on final behind Centurion, go all the way to the green dot ... Very good. Twin behind RV, land on the orange dot. RV at the Northeast corner start right turn onto base for 27 following the Bonanza.

And on and on all day like this! It's a wonderful experience. I hope you stay at least a couple days and make the most of it. You will probably go back again. Every one of my eight planes took me there.

An example of the hood used in IFR training

Chapter Fifteen

May 21, 1977
IFR RATING — WHO NEEDS IT?

My logbook on this date shows 410 hours total time to date. Since I bought the 182 a year earlier, I had been taking more and more business flights, and the distances are greater. I also had to park the plane at a destination two times and rent a car to return home, after VFR conditions eroded.

I really hated the times when weather turned sour and I had to do some scud-running to complete a trip. *Flying* magazine has printed lots of stories about unhappy endings when VFR turns to IFR.

When I started seriously considering an IFR rating, there was a pleasant surprise waiting. I found that my military background qualified me for IFR instruction that would be paid by the GI Bill for veterans. That made the decision easier! So, on this date in 1977, I started IFR training.

The flight part is lots of fun. Learning to fly "under the hood" is a real challenge. On each flight, as soon as we were airborne, I was told to put on the training hood, which blocks outside vision and limits the pilot to see the instruments only. Finally, I get to use instruments on my panel that I've not used before! The one I still chuckle about is the ADF.

In 1977, the proper use of an ADF was part of the flight exam, and after I learned how to use it and passed the IFR flight exam, I never used it again for navigation. I did, however, find it great as a radio.

A weekly flight lesson was recommended by my instructor, and that was good advice. Some weeks, we would fly more than once. Between April and September, I logged 35.3 training hours in the air.

The hard part for me was the ground study. Learning the endless rules of the IFR system made me cross-eyed. A good student I've never been, and after a day at my dealership, I would come home to study the rules and promptly fall asleep! This wasn't working at all. I was making poor progress and my instructor suggested I attend an IFR training seminar. That turned out to be the solution.

May 14, 1977
DRINKING FROM A FIRE HOSE!

The concentrated two-day IFR seminar designed to help pilots pass the written exam was held in Green Bay. I flew there and found the time and investment was well worth it. They obviously had experience teaching other pilots with the same problem I was having. The instructors stuffed knowledge down our throats until it came out our ears. Two days later, I sat for the exam and, WHOOPEE! I passed it. What a relief that was!

September 7, 1977
THE FINAL TEST — IN ACTUAL IFR CONDITIONS

This was a good day. I much preferred the time I had been training in actual IFR weather conditions as opposed to flying "under the hood." It was more realistic. On this date, my flight exam turned out to be in actual IFR conditions, and Wally Pratt signed off for my IFR ticket! About six months had passed since May, and my logbook showed 494 hours. Suddenly, I felt my airplane was much more useful in our business.

SOME GOOD ADVICE

A pilot friend suggested I file IFR for every trip, long or short, the same as commercial airline pilots do, to get practice using the system. I did that, and it was excellent advice. Filing the flight plan and copying the clearances became easier the more I did it. Competing in the same airspace with airliners can be intimidating, and as I used the system more I felt comfortable in it.

I actually laughed at myself on one trip, when there was a lot of airliner conversation near O'Hare and I was going into Palwaukee. The airline pilots sometime talk in a lower tone, sort of impressive and authoritative. I found myself talking lower, as if I had 200 passengers aboard. (I got over that habit!)

> *The IFR ticket was about the best life insurance I ever had in the air.*

Even before I got the IFR ticket, I felt like night flying was more IFR than VFR, and tended to avoid it, even though it's a great time to be in the air. After receiving my new rating, I really enjoyed night trips. It's always amazing how the presence of other planes stands out at night. Sometimes it is really hard to tell if the light is a plane or a star. There is magic up there!

Looking back over 40 years of flying, the IFR ticket was about the best life insurance I ever had in the air.

Aircraft Purchase/Sales Agreement

ehF/Flugskoli Akureyrar, THIS AGREEMENT is entered into this _28_ day of __January__ __2008__, by and between
_____ (the "Buyer"), a(n) _____ (individual(s), corporation, partnership, or LLC) whose principal
address is __Hofsbot 4 600 Akureyri Iceland__ ; and __Paul Wallem__ (the "Seller"), a
(n) __an__ (individual(s), corporation, partnership, or LLC) whose principal address is
__5109 Farmington Close, Rockford, IL 61114__.

IN WITNESS WHEREOF, in consideration of the premises, the mutual covenants contained herein, and other good and valuable
consideration, the sufficiency of which is hereby acknowledged, the parties do hereby agree as follows:

1. Sale of Aircraft. Seller agrees to sell to Buyer and Buyer agrees to purchase from Seller the following Aircraft (the "Aircraft"):

Aircraft Make __Fairchild__
Aircraft Model __M-62A__
Aircraft Year __1941__
Aircraft Registration Number __1941N__
Aircraft Serial Number __T41-1184__
Aircraft shall be equipped as follows ____
__King KLX135, King KN76 w/encoder, intercom, starter,__
__generator, NAV lights, maintenance manuals__

Seller warrants that Seller holds legal title to the Aircraft and that title will be transferred to Buyer free and clear of any liens,
claims, charges, or encumbrances. Upon delivery of the Aircraft and payment of the balance of the purchase price, in
accordance with this Agreement, Seller shall execute a bill of sale granting good and marketable title to the Aircraft.

2. Consideration. It is agreed that the price of the Aircraft is __73 Thousand__ Dollars ($__73,000__) and is due on**and part**
delivery of the Aircraft. All monies paid in accordance with this Agreement will be made by cash, cashier's check, certified check,**before**
wire transfer, or equivalent.

*A template provided by the AOPA website was used for
the sale of my PT-19 to a museum in Iceland.*

Chapter Sixteen

WHAT MIGHT HAVE BEEN

Back in Chapter Seven, I wrote about Plane Number Seven, the PT-19, going to a Texas buyer on May 6, 2008. That was actually the second time I had sold the plane that year. The first "sale" was quite a learning experience for me.

On January 20, 2008, I had an agreement to sell the PT-19 to a museum in Iceland. All necessary export requirements were met, with almost 40 emails, faxes and UPS shipments occurring between the first contact on December 11, 2007 and the final email on January 30, when the deal fell apart.

The entire process was fascinating, and who knows? You may buy or sell a plane outside the country and will be more familiar with the process after reading the following exchanges, which are edited to provide an overview of this export transaction. I received an email sales lead from *controller.com*.

December 11, 2007

Re: Fairchild PT-19 $61,000.

Iceland: Hi I interest to the PT-19. pls give info of center section. I am EAA member.

December 11, 2007

Me: I am providing you details on renovation history and pictures.

December 13, 2007

Iceland: received photos. can you fax papers of maintenance and restoration?

December 20, 2007

Iceland: Hi - we have questions about your PT. As we are both EAA members I hope you are willing to answer details honestly ... tell overall appearance, interior appearance, fabric, also size of center section if too wide for 8' container. I'm working on shipping.

December 21, 2007

Me: Sending you all details requested UPS.

December 23, 2007

Iceland: We have possibly B-747 coming Chicago, can open nose for loading, how far you from Chicago?

December 23, 2007

Me: One hour from O'Hare Chicago.

December 24, 2007

Me: I have logbooks from renovation, list of 13 original owners, FAA record of airplane history since went to the military in 1943. How close are you to the Arctic Circle?

December 30, 2007

Iceland: Hi, pictures and measurements you sent great, and very interested. We meeting this weekend on freight. Too wide for 8' container, maybe B-747. Iceland is short of the Arctic Circle we can take a flight from my town to a small island Guernsey and step on the Arctic line.

December 31, 2007

Iceland: I ask you for quote on packing and shipping to

NY and NY to Iceland.

January 2, 2008
Me: Google Emery Air, Inc. Rockford Il. They offer complete service of dismantling, packing and shipping small planes.

January 19, 2008
Iceland: We decided to go ahead purchase your PT-19. Your price $61,000. We will agree to $60,000. Send AOPA sales agreement. We will pay deposit on Monday and make AOPA escrow. $5000 to your bank.

January 20, 2007
Me: My ABA routing number is _____. AOPA Selling Agreement faxed today.

January 29, 2008
Iceland: We have some struggling in our group because stock market crisis ... our currency Icelandic Krona is in free-fall down 15% since our discussions. Will go forward with agreement.

January 29, 2008
Me: We will wrap and store in luggage compartment all logbooks, overhaul manuals and FAA CD aircraft history. I have faxed agreement.

January 30, 2008
Iceland: Hi Paul we show up to have problem in financing now. I called back again - bank is denying financing. I so deeply sorry. Terribly sorry after all discussions between us. This was right aircraft for us. So deeply sorry again. Best regards.

When I received that last "Dear John" email, I was quite surprised. The photos of their museum were impressive, and I had actually talked to my good friend, United Captain Jerry Pitts, about visiting Iceland after my plane got there.

But think back to 2008. Financial markets worldwide tumbled, banks closed, mortgages got called, and it was even worse in Iceland. Their three largest commercial banks stopped lending.

This was an interesting experience, though. The lesson learned again is no deal is done until the money arrives!

February 25, 2008

Iceland: Hope you sold your plane. Best regards.

The AOPA *Guide to Aircraft Importing and Exporting* was very helpful. I downloaded all 25 pages and referred to it throughout the discussions.

April 8, 2016

THE REST OF THE STORY

Would you believe this same PT-19 was just purchased by Lone Star Flight Museum of Galveston? So, this fine old military trainer does end up in a museum after all.

→ Rule of the Air ←

Always try to keep the number of landings you make equal to the number of takeoffs you've made.

> *Any idiot can get an airplane off the ground, but an aviator earns his keep by bringing it back anytime, anywhere, under any circumstances that man and God can dream up.*
>
> — Walter Cunningham,
> *The All-American Boys*, 1977

Planes and their prices have changed a lot since this ad in a 1928 edition of Aviation *magazine.*

Chapter Seventeen

HOW MUCH DO AIRPLANES COST?

My passengers have often asked this question. I struggled for an answer, because there are so many variables. So let's compare some of the planes I've owned with prices currently on the Internet.

Of course, since my first purchase in 1974, prices on virtually everything have increased substantially. In the case of aircraft, however, another factor enters in. Huge advances in technology have made available a lot of sophisticated equipment that has made flying safer, easier, more precise, and harder for pilots to get lost!

Here are some examples of cockpit technology that did not exist or were rare when I started flying: GPS, collision avoidance systems, engine monitors, radar, precise autopilots, and avionics packages that incorporate much of the above. Today's glass cockpits are a marvel to fly with. Noise-canceling headsets are a great advantage over the old ones.

Of course, all of that convenience and safety comes at a price. It is not unusual to add well over $100,000 to the price of a new airplane by installing equipment such as is described above. It's possible to add a parachute to certain models.

The price of used planes reflects the equipment onboard. My first plane was a 1974 Cessna 172. It was less than a year old and I paid $20,000 for it. In researching this book, I found a 1974 172 on the Internet for $90,000. Another was offered for $66,000, yet another for

$43,000, and so on. The difference is due to condition, hours used, and equipment. Hours on the engine is a very large factor because an engine overhaul can easily exceed $30,000. A buyer has to factor all these variables into a decision as to which airplane to buy.

A Cessna 182 Skylane like my second and eighth planes has more room, more power, and certainly costs more. I found a 15-year-old Skylane on the Internet for $207,000. Another one was three years old with a turbo, advertised for $449,000! (That's sort of serious money.)

A 1973 182, the same age as my second airplane, is advertised for $69,000. A new 182 will cost well over $400,000 and can easily reach into the $500,000 range. But fully equipped, it is a very capable and serious airplane.

A search for used Cessna T-210's, like my third and fifth planes, brought up choices on the Internet such as a 1977 model, the same year as my first 210, for $185,000. Another one advertised was asking $119,000. Again, the differences in price result from variations in condition, engine time, equipment, paint, etc. Cessna stopped building the 210 after 1985.

Aircraft in the six-passenger turbocharged category that are currently on the market can cost $800,000 or more when new. (To keep peace in the family, you may want to tell your spouse ahead of time that you are buying this one.)

Age is a minor factor in the pricing of used aircraft. Every plane must be re-certified annually as to airworthiness. An owner who might be tempted to skip this expense knows that his insurance is void if an accident occurs with an aircraft out of annual! He also risks being grounded by a ramp inspection.

Paul Wallem

Eddy Rickenbacker, following his first plane ride with Glenn Martin (the founder of Martin-Marietta) asked why his vertigo hadn't occurred during flight.
"It's because there is nothing to judge height by," Martin told him. "There's no edge to look over."

— from *The Aviators* by Winston Groom

"Home away from home:"
my Poplar Grove Airport hangar

Epilogue

I'M REMINISCING ... WANT TO LISTEN IN?

I'm sitting in my airplane-less hangar at Poplar Grove Airport. My last plane, love affair number eight, is now 30 miles away at Galt Airport (10C) with its new owner. Surrounding me, the hangar walls are covered with memories.

I spent 13 years with International Harvester Company, and from 1966 to 1968, I traveled 52 countries as the company's farm equipment export manager. The travel schedules for those years hang on the hangar wall. There are two incidents during that time that I will never forget.

On October 1, 1967, Elio Hernandez sat beside me en route from Miami to Lima, Peru. He was our South American product specialist. Elio was born in Cuba, and escaped years earlier on a small boat. His parents were still there, though, and he had not seen them for years. We overflew Cuba that day, and he looked down where his parents lived. My heart went out to him. Several years after that, he did find a way to see them again, and all these years later, Cuba is again open to Americans!

Just two weeks later, October 14, 1967, I flew from Tokyo to Taipei, Taiwan. We flew over the Mekong Delta in South Vietnam where the U.S. had thousands of troops at the time. As I looked down from 30,000 feet at that marshland, water everywhere, I wondered how they could fight in that mess.

Before I left Taipei on the 17th, I had the radio in my hotel room tuned to BBC, and heard that Major Don Holleder had been killed that day in South Vietnam. The announcer added that he had been an All-American on the 1954 West Point football team.

I still recall the great sadness I felt as I remembered my connection to Don. Ten years earlier in 1957, we had played 25th Division football at Schofield Barracks in Hawaii. Don and I were lieutenants, and he helped me, a novice right tackle, learn how to block better. Even though he had been named an All-American, had his picture on the cover of *Sports Illustrated* and was offered an NFL contract (he turned it down to serve in the Army), he treated everyone as equals.

I Googled Don's name, and a medic who was with him when he died said in an interview that Don had been leading a team of soldiers and medics into a battlefield to gather the wounded when he was cut down. He added that everyone liked and admired the Major, described as a "man of sacrifices." Sounded like he hadn't changed. Major Holledor was posthumously awarded the Silver Star for his actions, and in 1988, West Point named its indoor sports facility in his honor.

In 1968, I could no longer handle the travel, being away from my family so much, and bought the IH dealership in Belvidere, Illinois. The north wall of the hangar also is full of pictures of that dealership and the one we opened later in Plainfield, Wisconsin, with my friend Bill Kleckner. There are a lot of IH toy tractors and trucks on that wall, too.

My oldest child, Jeff, also worked for IH corporate and then joined me in the dealerships, so a lot of this north hangar wall holds memories for him, too, as well as for the rest of our family. Two other walls are devoted to photos and memorabilia that include our whole family.

The south side of the hangar is covered with photos of the "good old days" when this airport started. There is a great photo of founder and then-owner Dick Thomas in his green Waco UPF7 with Bob Collins in the front seat.

In later years, Dick's son and daughter-in-law, Steve and Tina Thomas, bought a beautiful Beech 18 from an English owner, and the pictures show us all on the taxiway as the ferry pilot brought it to Poplar Grove. That plane has become the mascot of C77!

One of my favorite pictures is of Steve in that Beech with Ken Morris and his pristine Spartan in close formation! Those two always fly (very) close formation. All eight of my airplanes are on the wall, too.

That wall also features timeline photos of Poplar Grove Vintage Wings and Wheels Museum, from 1996 through the grand opening. I was privileged to be one of the four founders of the museum, which sits on 10 acres of ground donated by Steve and Tina. Many hundreds of volunteers have built this great place. It gets better every day.

I'm still looking at that south wall, with a bookcase full of memories of my family. No one has been blessed more than I've been with a great wife, children and grandchildren. All of them have flown

The west wall of the hangar, where many of Cheryl Wallem's paintings are displayed

with me through the years, and have been polite and quiet through some of my more marginal landings.

I'll finish with the west wall. My daughter-in-law Cheryl is an art teacher and started making paintings of my planes even before she and Jeff were married. Through the years, she painted each of the first five planes, and those occupy the west wall. They are treasures of mine.

The east wall is a 40-foot door (where planes used to come and go). No pictures on that wall! We use the hangar for other purposes now, and who knows what the future will bring? It's a home away from home, as is the Poplar Grove Airport.

Thanks for joining me on this tour of memories.

→ Rule of the Air ←

Flying isn't dangerous. Crashing is what's dangerous.

There is no sport equal to that which aviators enjoy while being carried through the air on great white wings.
— Wilbur Wright

Glossary

AGL — above ground level

AILERON — the movable areas of a wing form that control or affect the roll of an aircraft by working opposite one another

AIRFOIL — the shape of a flying surface, principally a wing (side view)

ARTCC — air route traffic control center - facility established to provide air traffic control service to aircraft operating on IFR flight plans within controlled airspace

ATC — service operated by appropriate authority to promote safe, orderly and expeditious air traffic flow

ATIS — a recording that some airports broadcast in order to reduce frequency congestion: current weather, active runway information, NOTAMs, and other useful pieces of information

AIR SPEED INDICATOR — instrument measuring airspeed, not ground speed

ANGLE OF ATTACK — acute angle at which a moving airfoil meets the airstream

AOPA — Aircraft Owners and Pilots Association

CAP — Civil Air Patrol

CAT — clear air turbulence

CAVU — ceiling and visibility unlimited (ideal flying weather)

CLEAR — a shouted warning by pilot that he is about to start the engine

CONSTANT SPEED PROP — a hydraulically-controlled propeller that governs an engine at its optimum speed by the blade pitch being increased or decreased automatically

DEADSTICK — descending flight with engine and propeller stopped

DIHEDRAL — the acute angle, usually upward, between the wing of

an airplane and a horizontal cross-section line
DME — distance measuring equipment
DRAG — the resisting force exerted on an aircraft in its line of flight opposite in direction to its motion
ELEVATOR — the movable part of a horizontal airfoil which controls the pitch of an aircraft, the fixed part being the stabilizer
ELT — emergency locator transmitter
EMPENNAGE — an aircraft's tail group, includes rudder and fin, and stabilizer and elevator
FBO — fixed base operator
FLAP — a movable, usually hinged AIRFOIL set in the trailing edge of an aircraft wing
FLARE — a simple maneuver performed moments before landing in which the nose of an aircraft is pitched up to minimize the touchdown rate of speed
GLASS COCKPIT — said of an aircraft's control cabin which has all-electronic, digital and computer-based instrumentation, and GPS global positioning system
GROSS WEIGHT — total weight of an aircraft when fully loaded, including fuel, cargo and passengers, aka takeoff weight
GROUND SPEED — the actual speed that an aircraft travels over the ground
HANGAR — an enclosed structure for housing aircraft. It originated with lake-based floating homes of the original German zeppelins in which they were "hanged" from cables, which explains the erroneous, oft-seen spelling of "hanger."
IFR — instrument flight rules
ILS — instrument landing system
KNOT — one nautical mile, about 1.15 statute miles
MSL — mean sea level
NDB — non-directional beacon

NOTAMs (Notices to Airmen) — unclassified notices or advisories distributed by means of telecommunication that contain information concerning the establishment, conditions or change in any aeronautical facility, service, procedure or hazard, the timely knowledge of which is essential to personnel and systems concerned with flight

PATTERN — the path of aircraft traffic around an airfield, at an established height and direction

PIC — pilot in command

RUDDER — the movable part of a vertical airfoil which controls the yaw of an aircraft

SCUD — a low, foglike cloud layer

SIDESLIP — a movement of an aircraft in which a relative flow of air moves along the lateral axis, resulting in a sideways movement from a projected flight path, especially a downward slip toward the inside of a banked turn

SIGMET — Significant Meteorological Information, is a weather advisory that contains meteorological information concerning the safety of all aircraft, including severe icing, and severe or extreme turbulence.

SKID — too shallow a bank in a turn, causing an aircraft to slide outward from its ideal turning path

SLIP — too steep a bank in a turn, causing an aircraft to slide inward from its ideal turning path

SMOH — since major overhaul

SQUAWK — a four-digit number dialed into his transponder by a pilot to identify his aircraft to air traffic controllers

STABILIZER — the fixed part of a horizontal airfoil that controls the pitch of an aircraft, the movable part being the elevator

STALL — (1) sudden loss of lift when the angle of attack increases to a point where the flow of air breaks away from a wing or airfoil, causing it to drop (2) A maneuver initiated by the steep raising of an aircraft's nose, resulting in a loss of velocity and an abrupt drop

TOUCH AND GO — landing practice in which an aircraft does not make a full stop after a landing, but proceeds immediately to another take-off

UNICOM — universal communication, a common radio frequency used at uncontrolled (non-tower) airports for pilot communication

USEFUL LOAD — the weight of crew, passengers, fuel, baggage and ballast, generally excluding emergency or portable equipment and ordnance

VERTICAL STABILIZER — the fixed part of a vertical airfoil that controls the yaw of an aircraft

VENTURI TUBE — a small, hourglass-shaped metal tube, usually set laterally on a fuselage in the slipstream to create suction for gyroscopic panel instruments

VFR — visual flight rules

VFR ON TOP — flight in which a cloud ceiling exists but modified visual flight rules are in effect if the aircraft travels above the cloud layer

VSI — vertical speed indicator

YAW — Yaw moves the nose of the aircraft from side to side. A positive yaw, or heading angle, moves the nose to the right. The rudder is the primary control of yaw.

YOKE — the control wheel of an aircraft, akin to a car's steering wheel

---

→ Rule of the Air ←

It's always better to be down here wishing you were up there,
than up there wishing you were down here.

Acknowledgments

My wife Joan, children Jeff, Linda and Steve Wallem and their families; Steve and Tina Thomas, Jerry Pitts, Bob Kemp, Lee Hilbert, Ken Morris, Lorraine Morris, Corinne Joy Brown, Coyle Schwab, Jerry Lagerloef, Phill Wolfe, Orion Samuelson, Gloria Samuelson, Steve Langdon, Frank Herdzina, Ed Meyers, Jon McGinty of *Northwest Quarterly Magazine*, and Diane Montiel and Steve Alexander of Bantry Bay Publishing. Without Diane and Steve, I would not have attempted this.

Photo: Jon McGinty

About the Author

Paul Wallem is a retired pilot after 40 years in the air, but remains an active, passionate supporter of Poplar Grove Airport (C77), Poplar Grove Vintage Wings and Wheels Museum, which he co-founded, and is a member of EAA Chapter 1414.

After graduating from the University of Illinois, he received a commission in the U.S. Army and headed the military police detachment, 25th Infantry Division. Paul then held five management positions with International Harvester, the last being Worldwide Manager of Farm Equipment Export Sales, with travels though 52 countries.

Paul left to open his own IH dealerships in Illinois and Wisconsin and operated them for 17 years before creating Wallem Associates in Rockford, a financial planning firm. His son Jeff, a partner in that business, continues to operate it. His daughter, Linda, is a creator of TV shows in Los Angeles, and son Stephen is a stage and TV performer in Manhattan.

Paul and Joan live in Rockford, Ilinois. Until recently, Joan has been active nationally with Phi Mu Foundation, and locally with a college and several hospital foundations.

Paul's aviation articles have been published in *Ranch* magazine and *Atlantic Flyer*. He welcomes your comments and stories. You can contact him at pwallem@aol.com.

When once you have tasted flight, you will forever walk the earth with your eyes turned skyward, for there you have been, and there you will always long to return.
— Leonardo da Vinci

Other titles from Bantry Bay Publishing

You Can't Dream Big Enough by Orion Samuelson

Stories from the Heartland by Max Armstrong

A Little More Les by Steve King and Johnnie Putman

50 Years of Disruptive Innovation by Jon Kinzenbaw

Wait Wait ... I'm Not Done Yet! by Carl Kasell

If Not for the Perfect Stranger -- Heartwarming and Healing Stories of Kindness from the 2013 Boston Marathon

Heart and Hustle by Frank Catalanotto

Backstage Past by Barry Fey

To contact the publisher, please email
bantrybaypublishing@gmail.com.